# Landscapes
## color by numbers

Martin Sanders and David Woodroffe

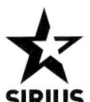
SIRIUS

This edition published in 2020 by Sirius Publishing, a division of
Arcturus Publishing Limited,
26/27 Bickels Yard, 151–153 Bermondsey Street,
London SE1 3HA

Copyright © Arcturus Holdings Limited

All rights reserved. No part of this publication may be reproduced,
stored in a retrieval system, or transmitted, in any form or by any
means, electronic, mechanical, photocopying, recording or otherwise,
without written permission in accordance with the provisions of the
Copyright Act 1956 (as amended). Any person or persons who do any
unauthorised act in relation to this publication may be liable to criminal
prosecution and civil claims for damages.

ISBN: 978-1-78828-548-3
CH005580NT
Supplier 29, Date 0220, Print Run 10128

Printed in China

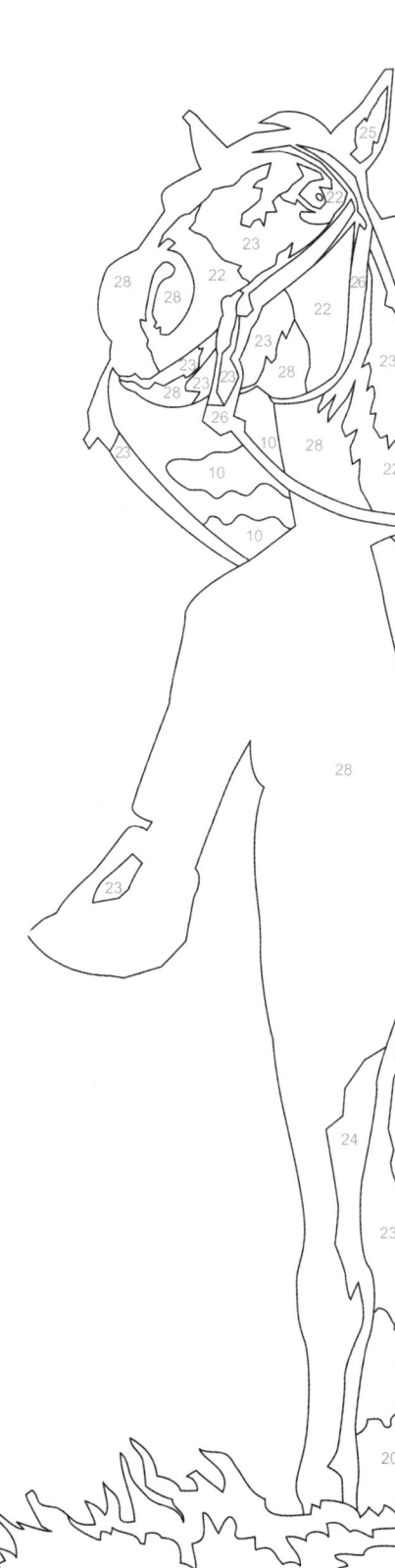

# Introduction

The earth's landscapes are some of its greatest wonders. From sun-seared deserts and freezing mountains where only the toughest survive, to coral reefs and rainforests swarming with life, landscapes are fascinating in their variety. This collection of color-by-number landscapes reflects that diversity, showing coastal views, dramatic waterfalls and mountains, safari scenes and bucolic country panoramas. Some images portray the impact of man on the landscape, such as the beautiful rice paddies carved out of a Chinese mountainside or the ancient stone circle at Stonehenge; others show wild places like the Antarctic or salmon jumping in a North American river. You will also find landscapes that are instantly recognizable, like Mount Fuji, Ayers Rock, and Niagara Falls.

Each image is fully numbered so that, by following the key on the back cover flap, you can build up an impressive landscape scene. Match your pencils as closely as possible to the colors in the key—you can even label the pencils with numbers to make things easier. If there is no number that means the space should be left white or colored with a white pencil.

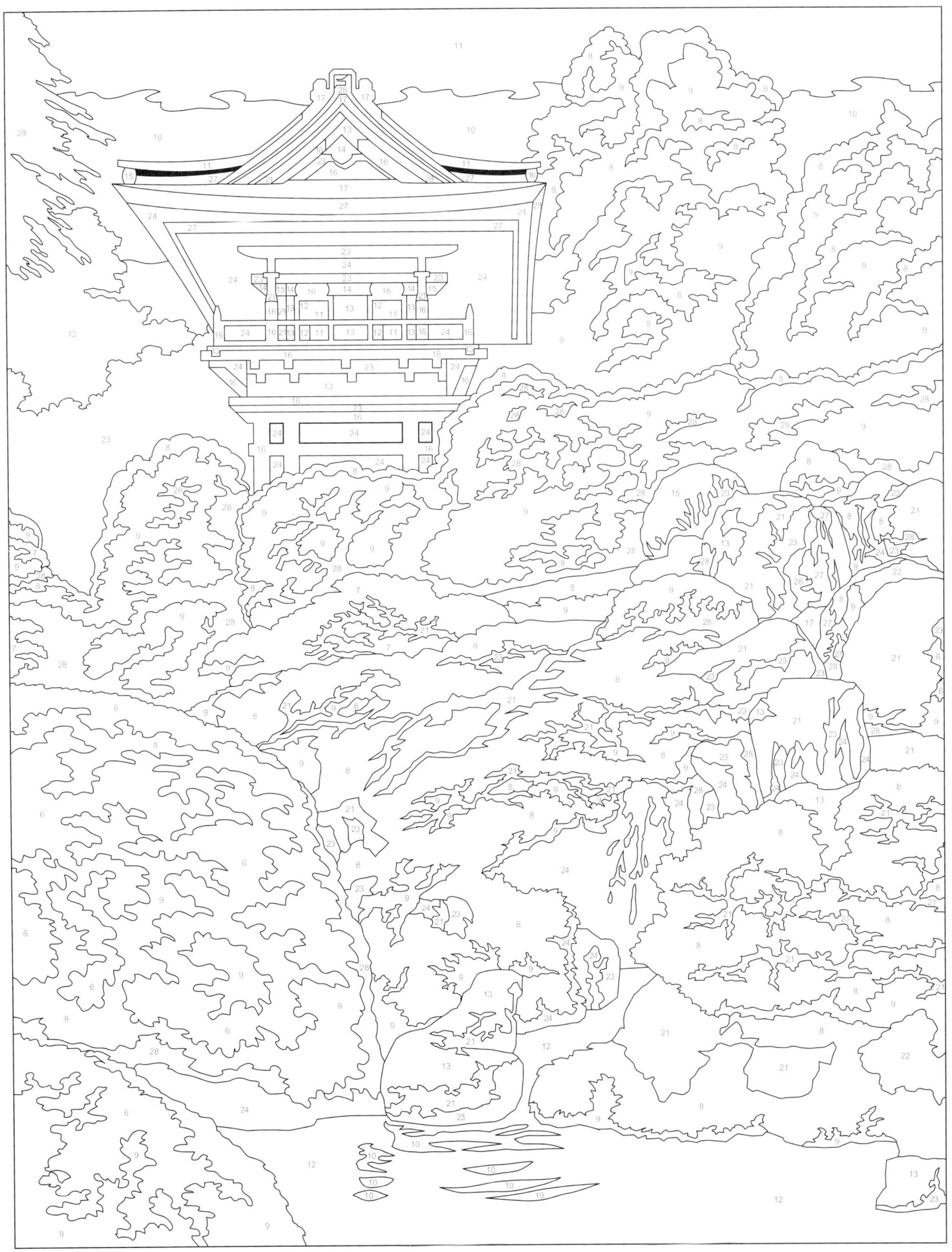

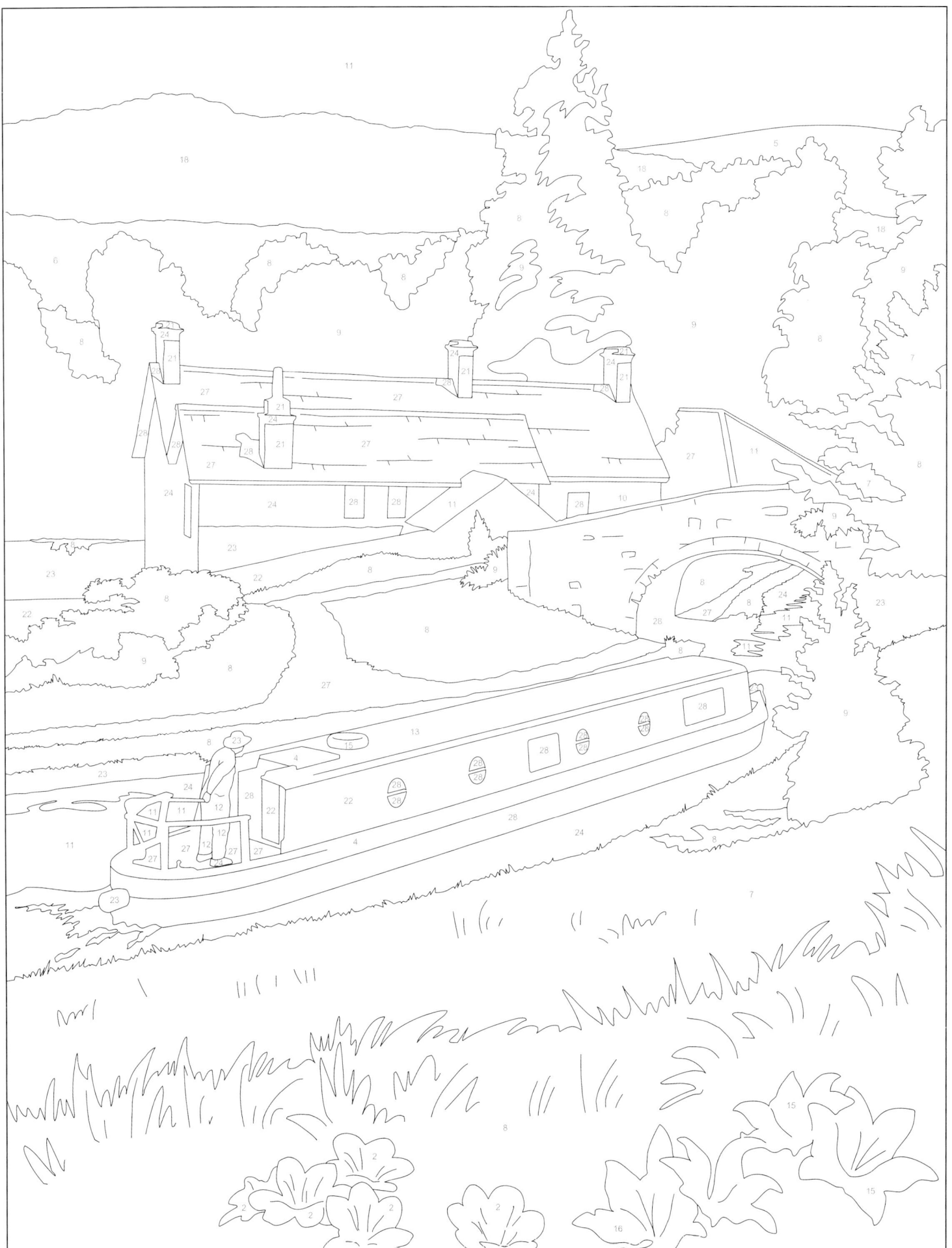

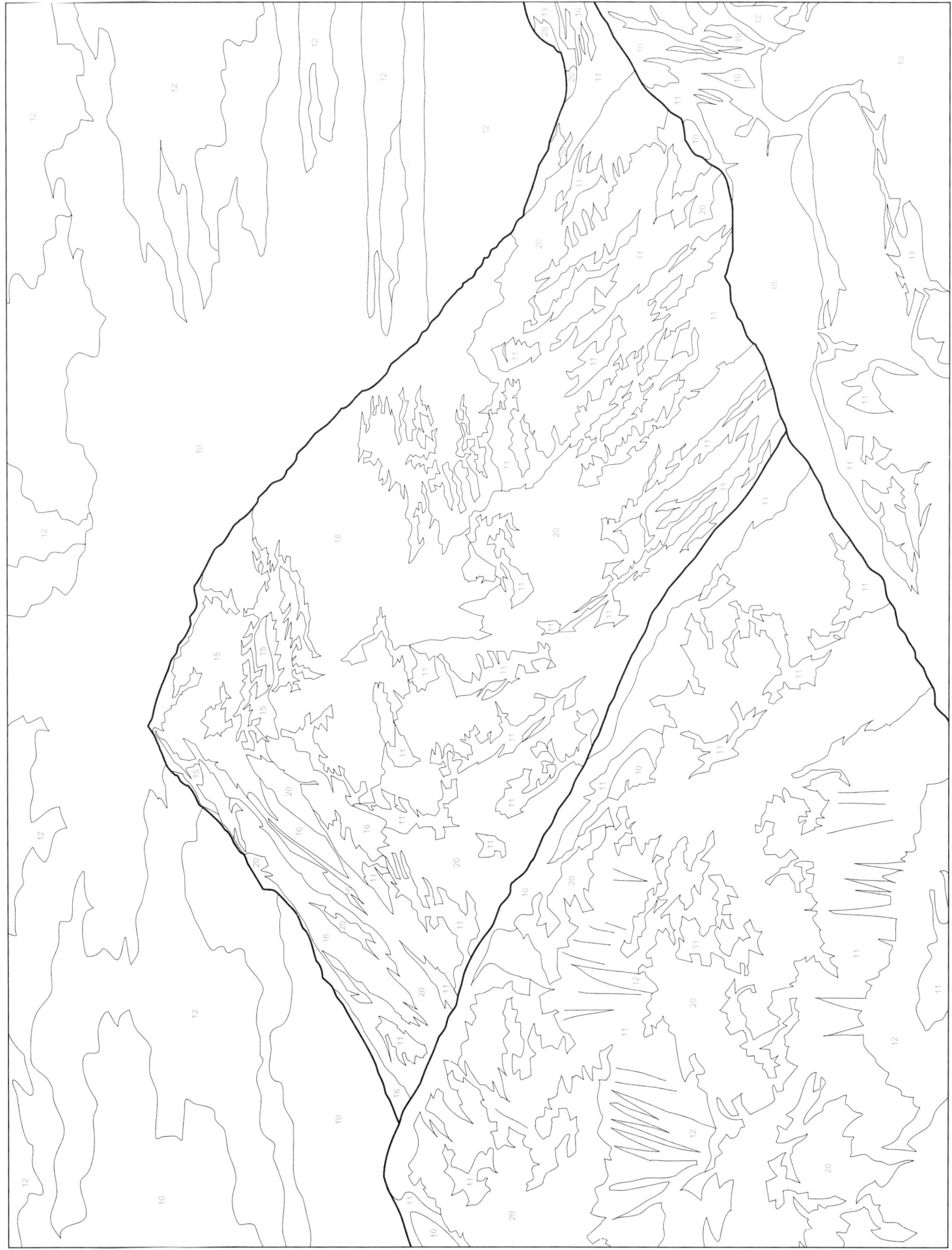

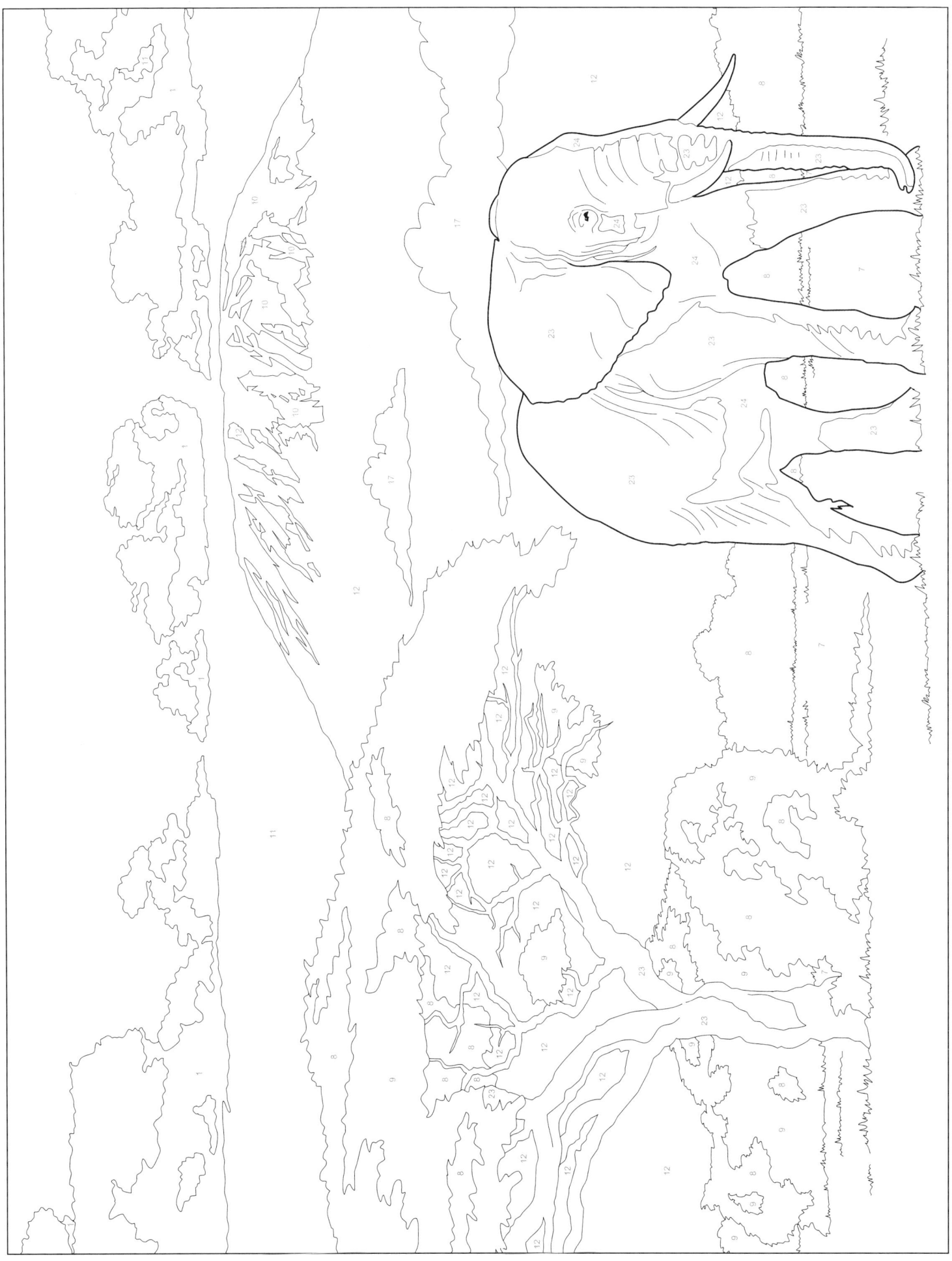

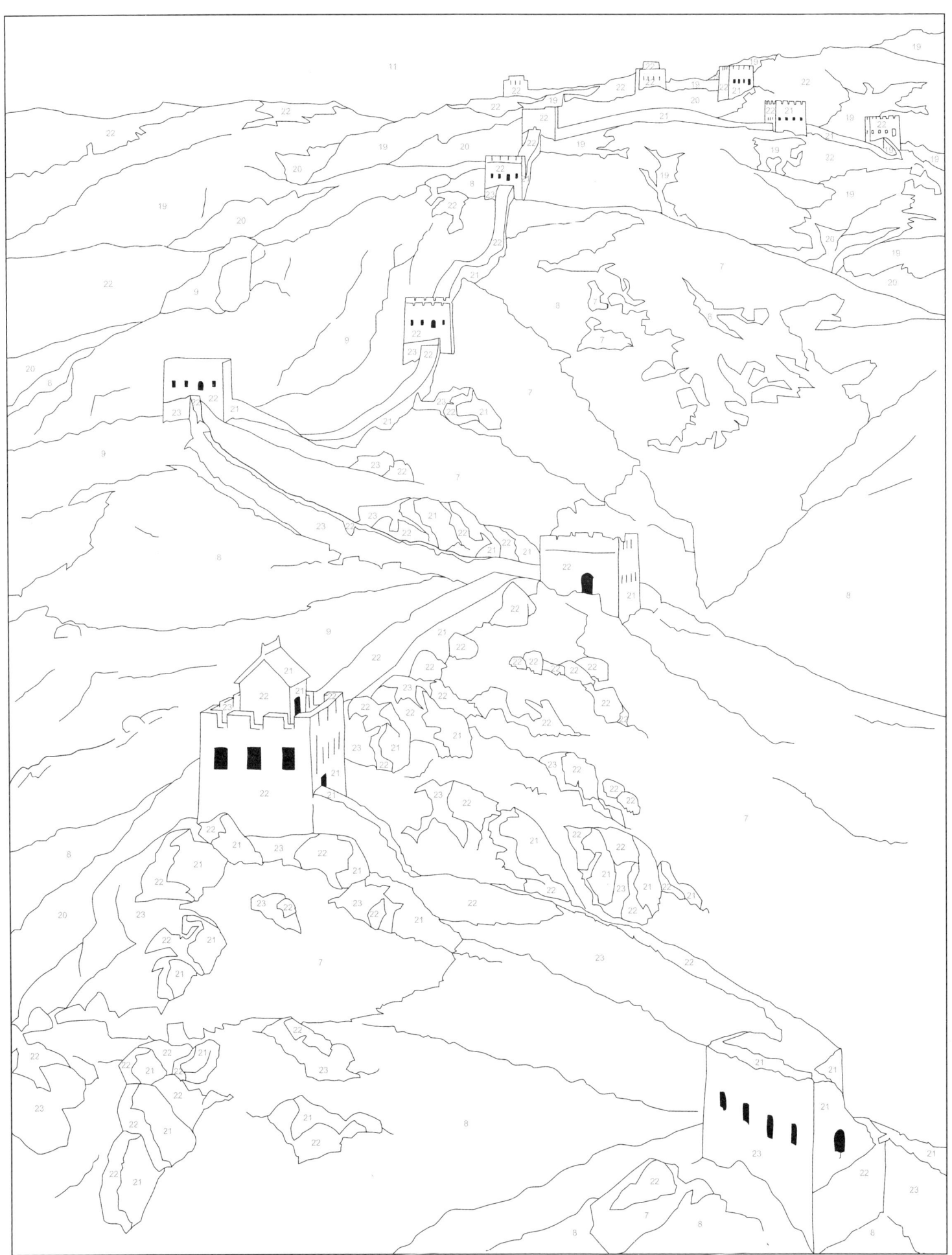

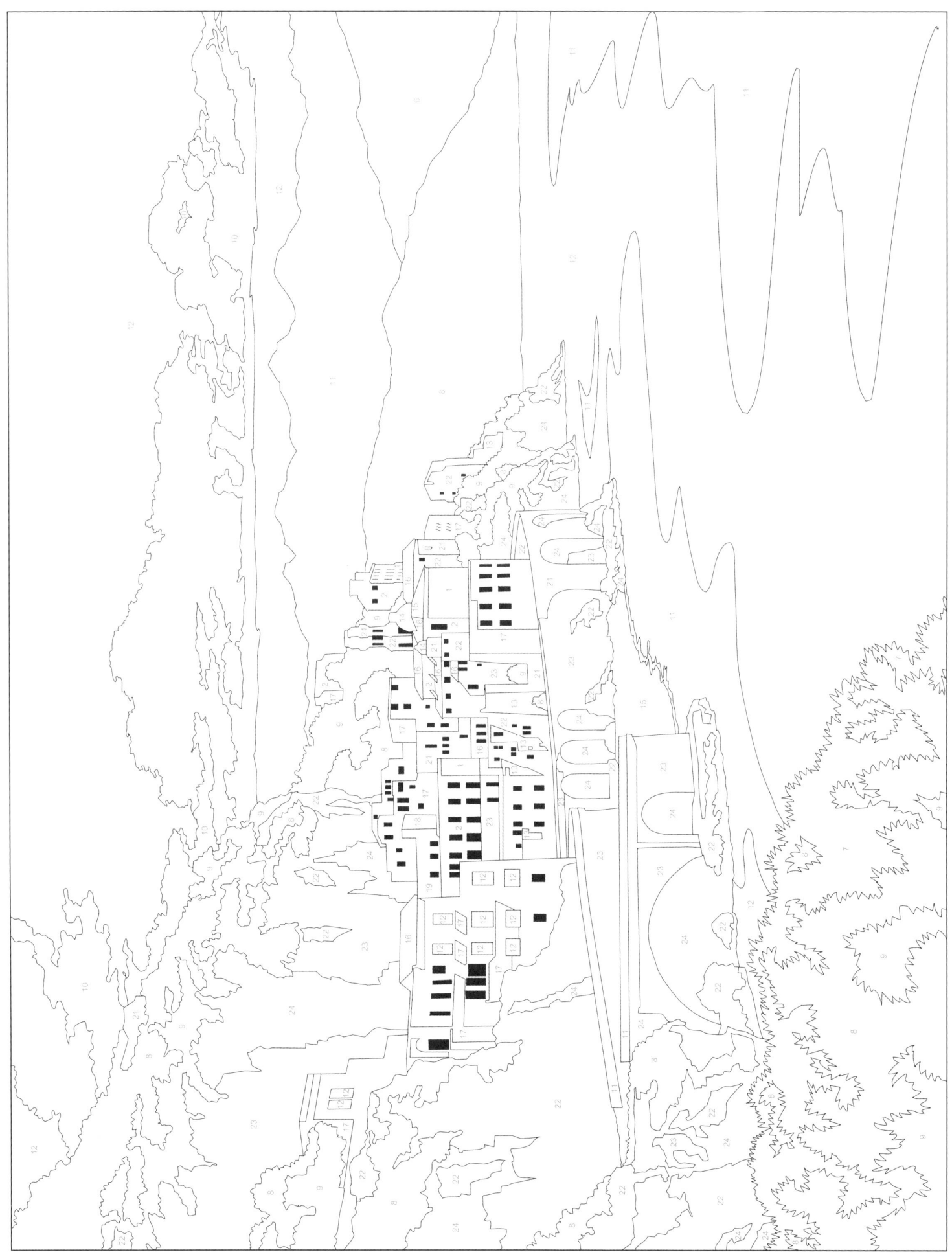

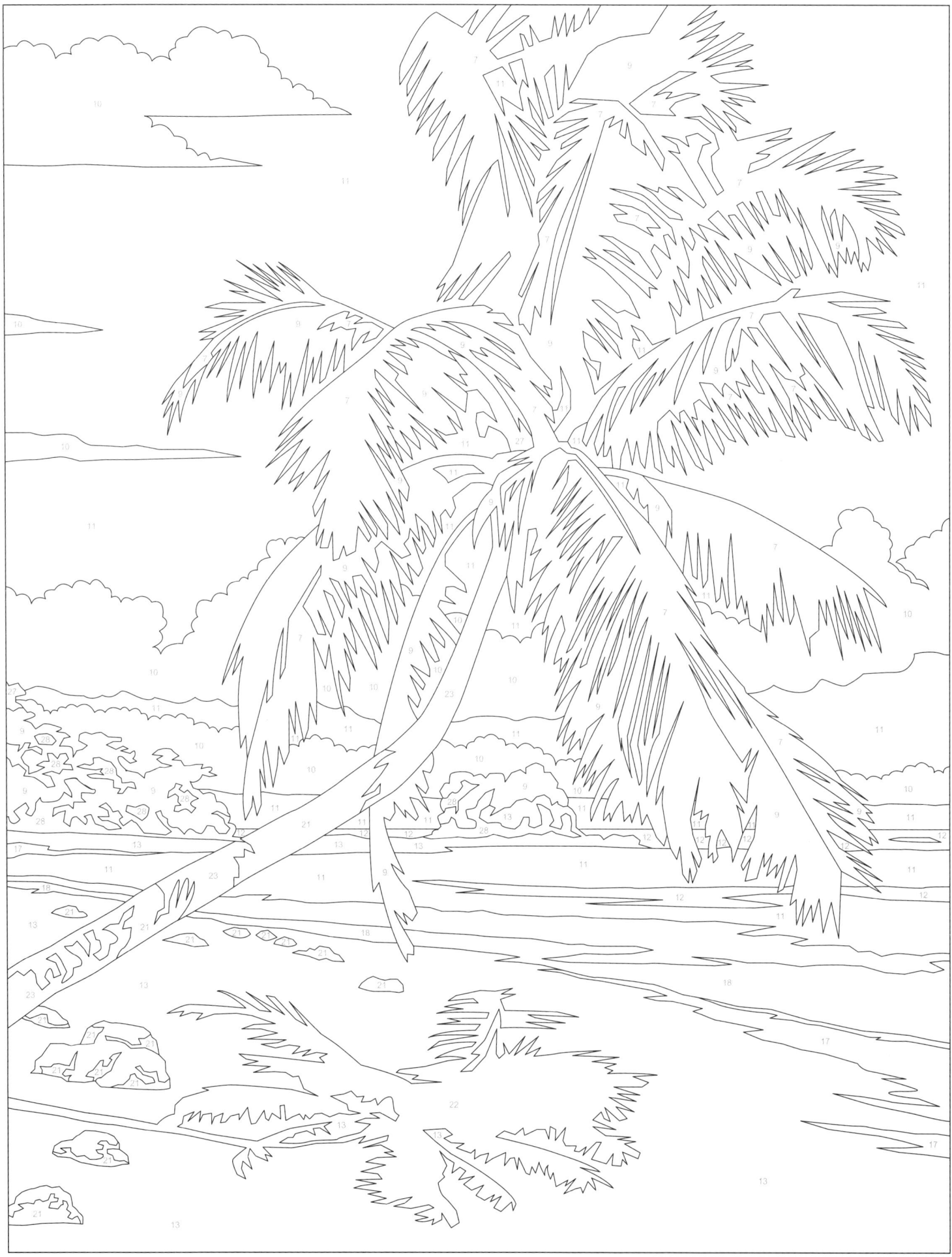

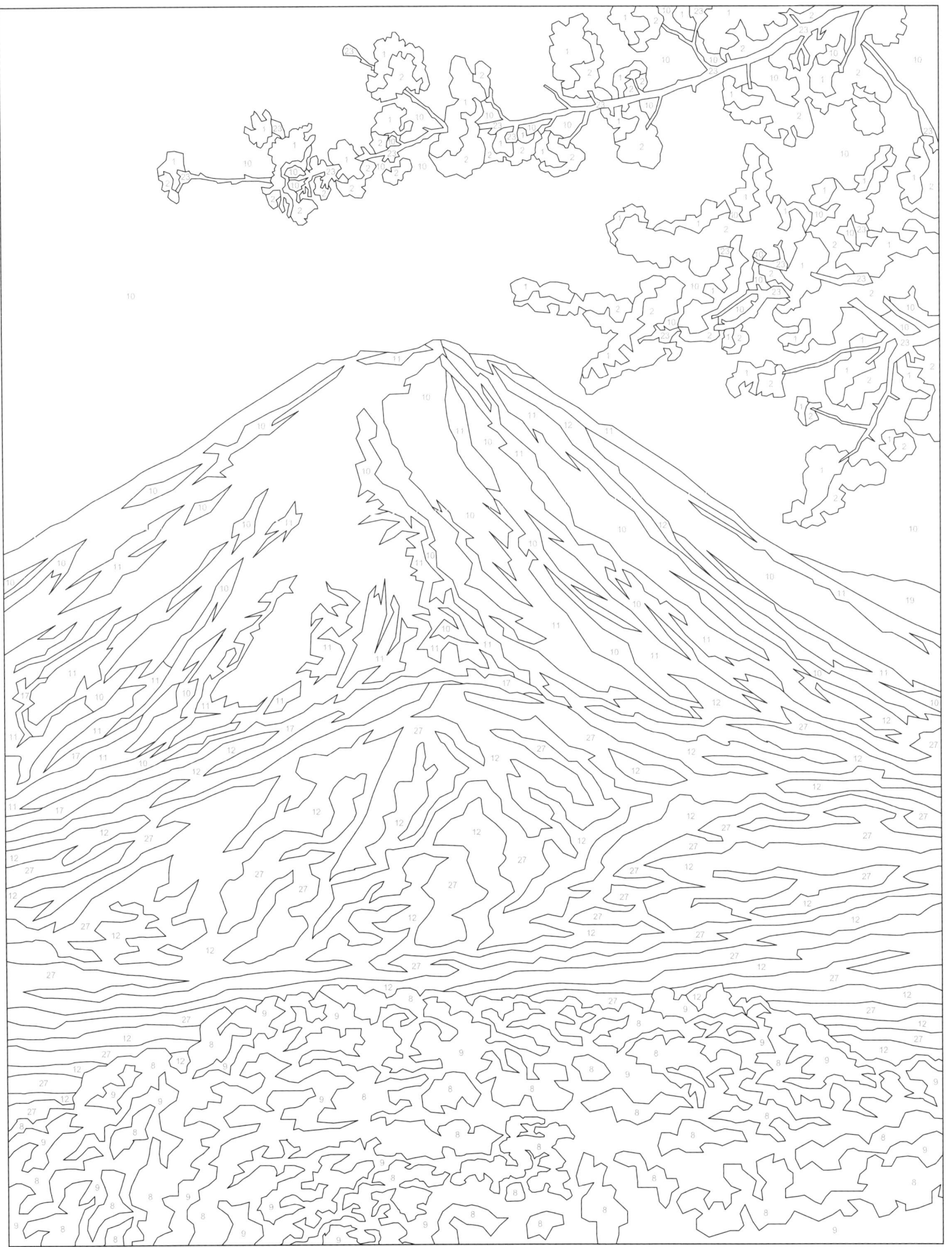

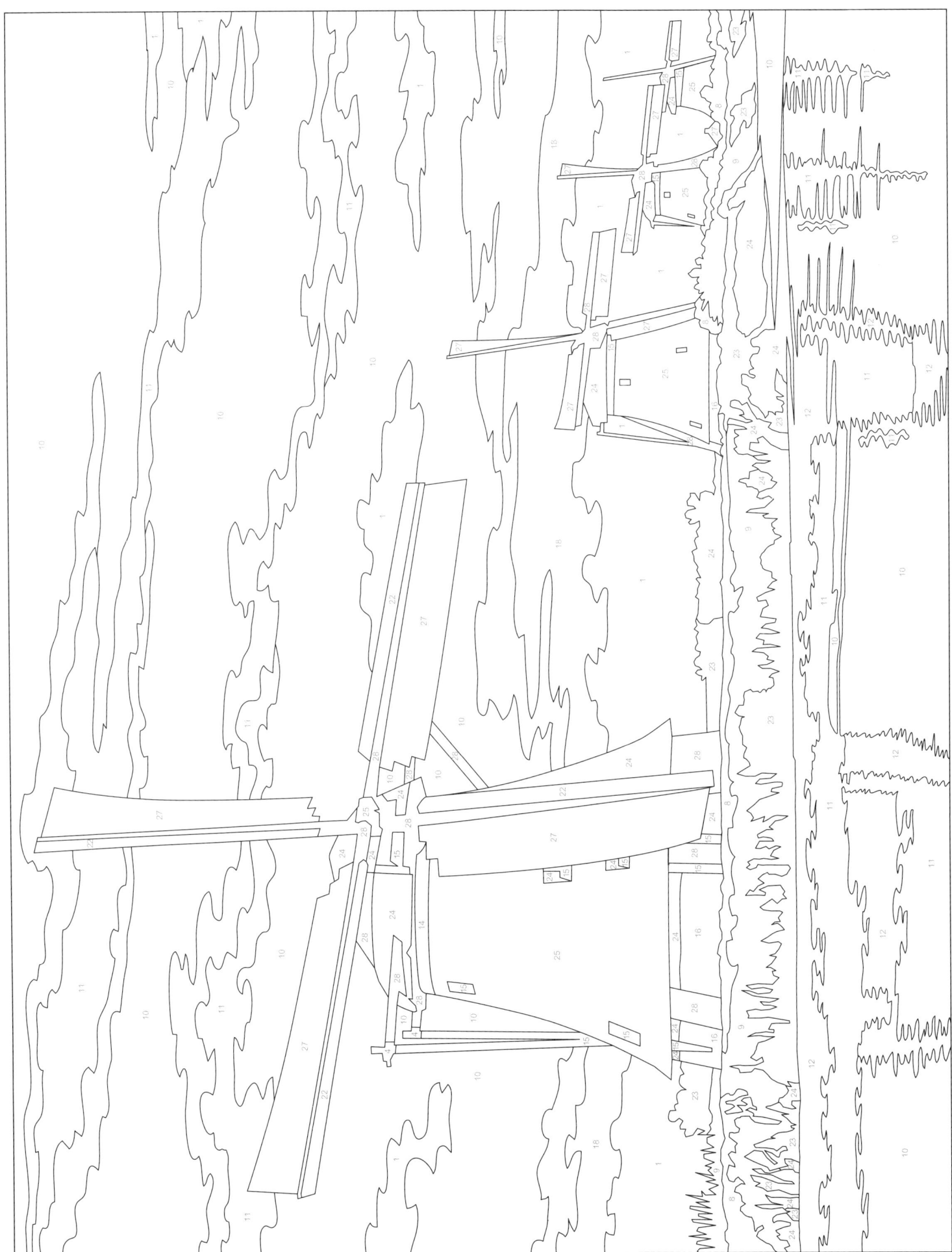

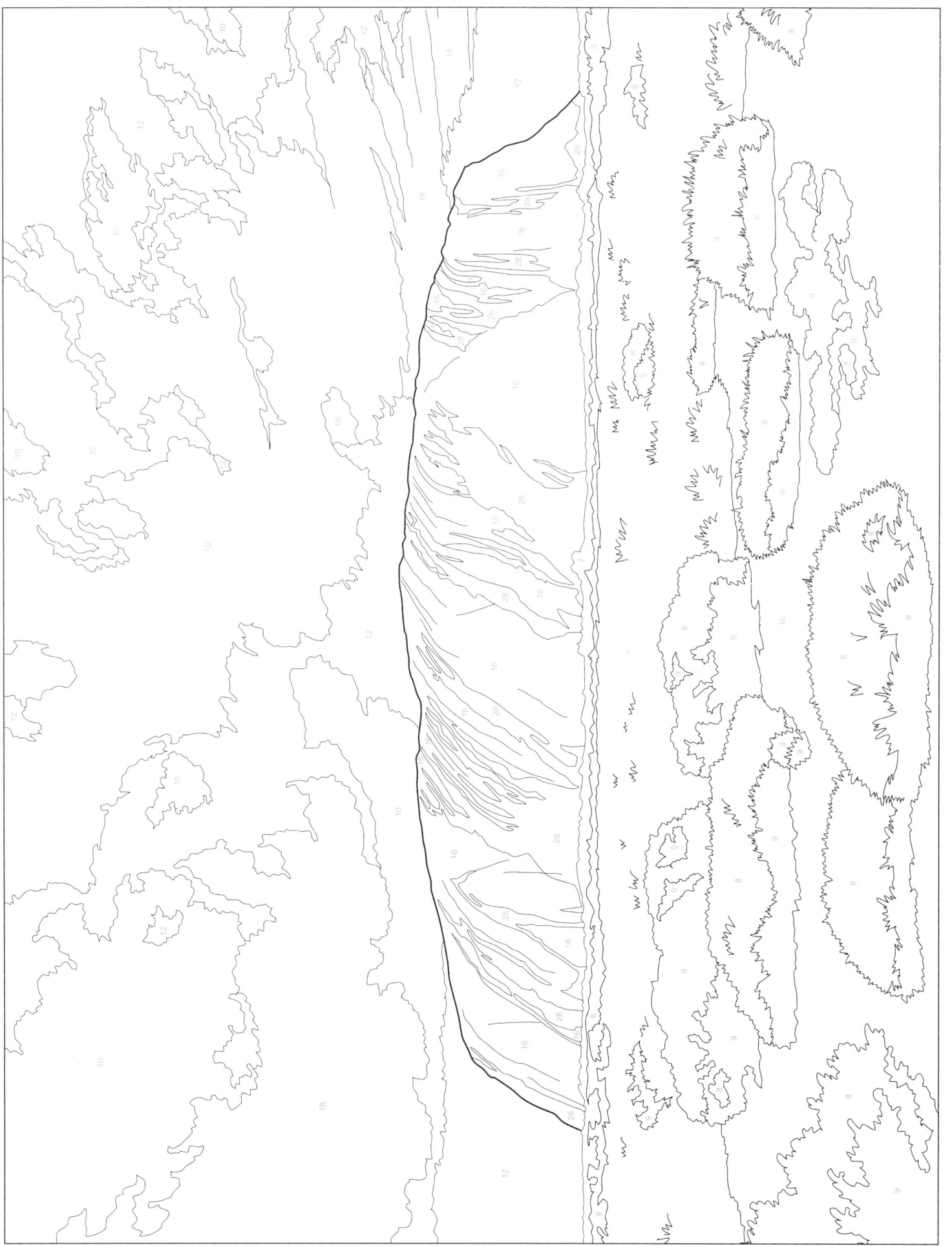

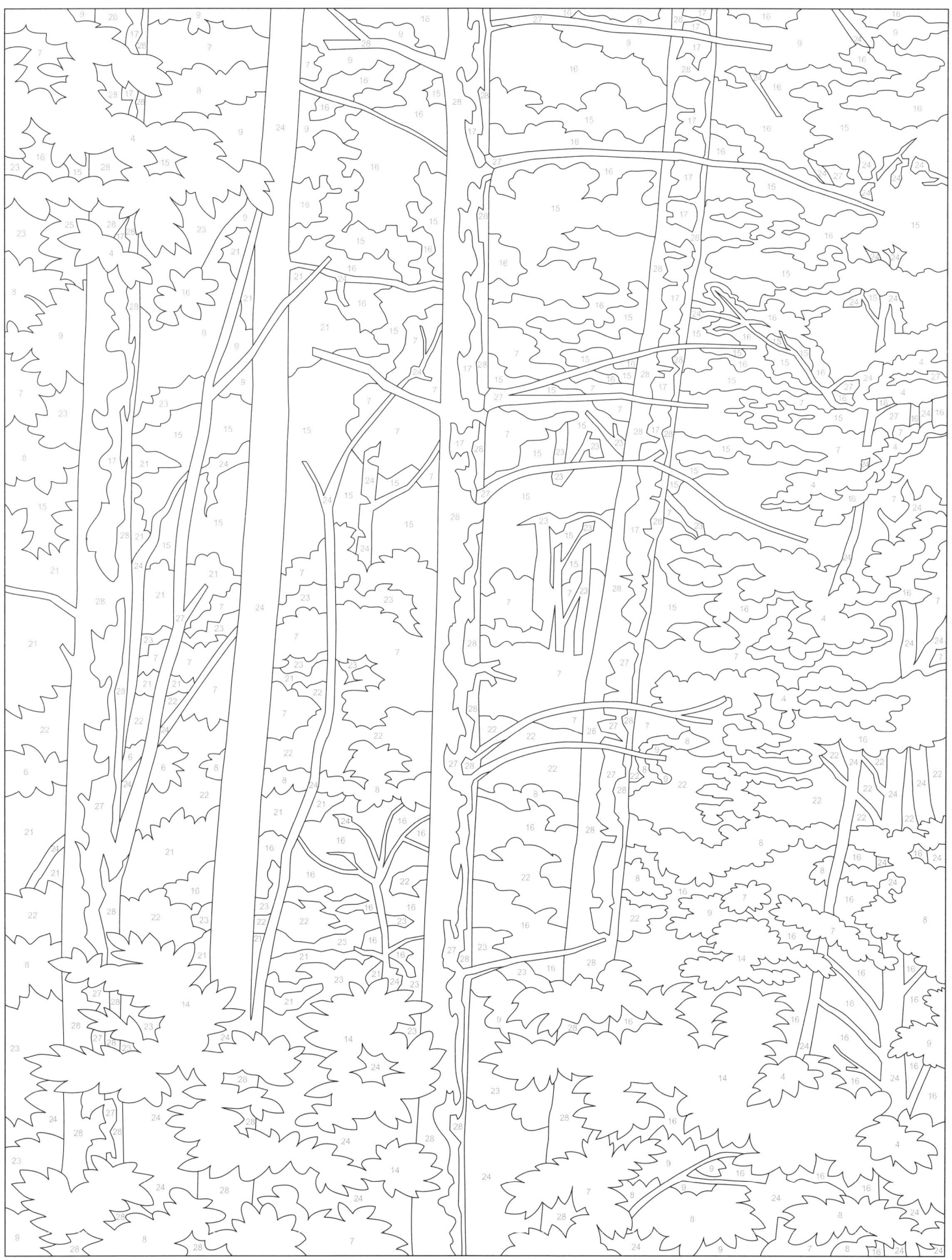

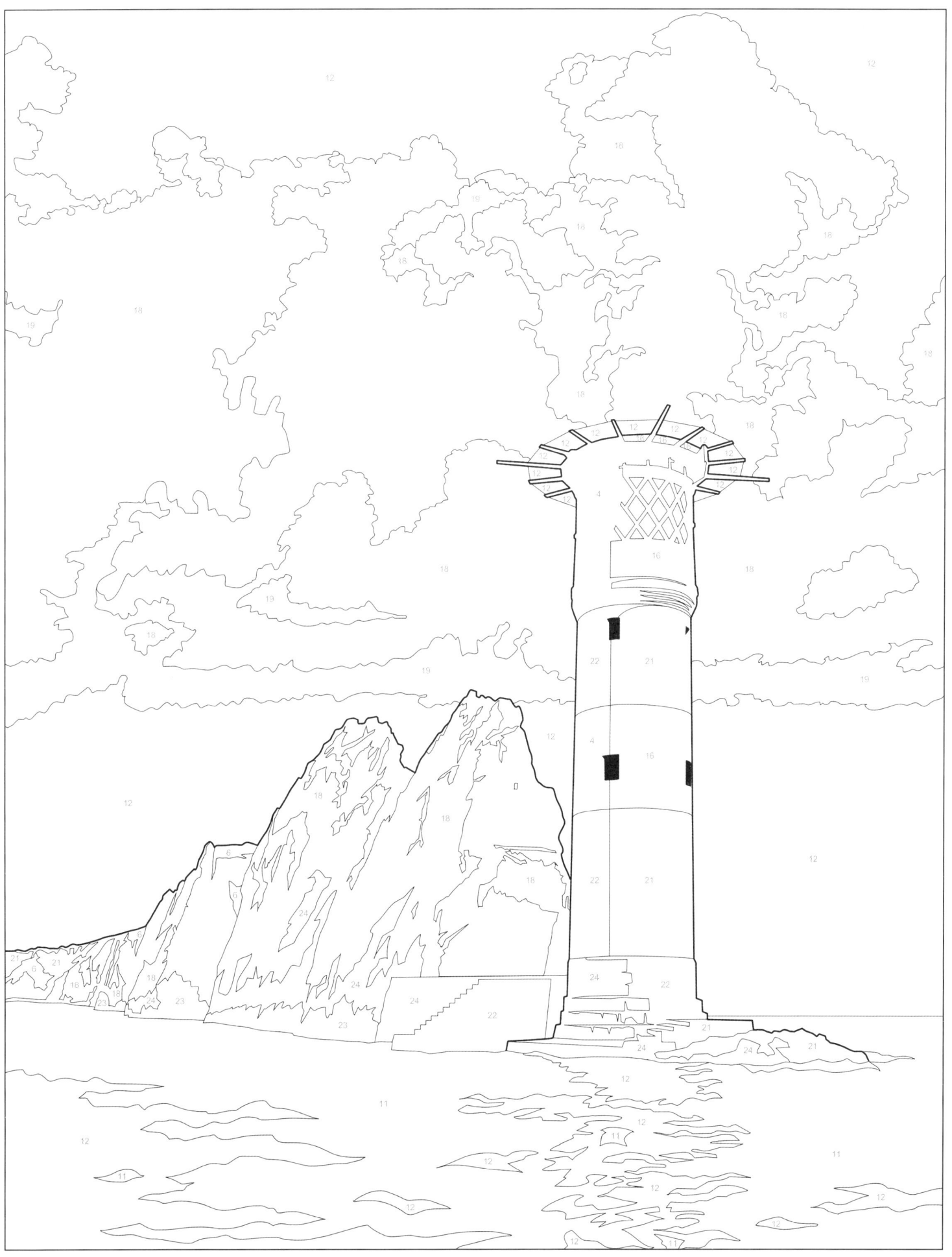

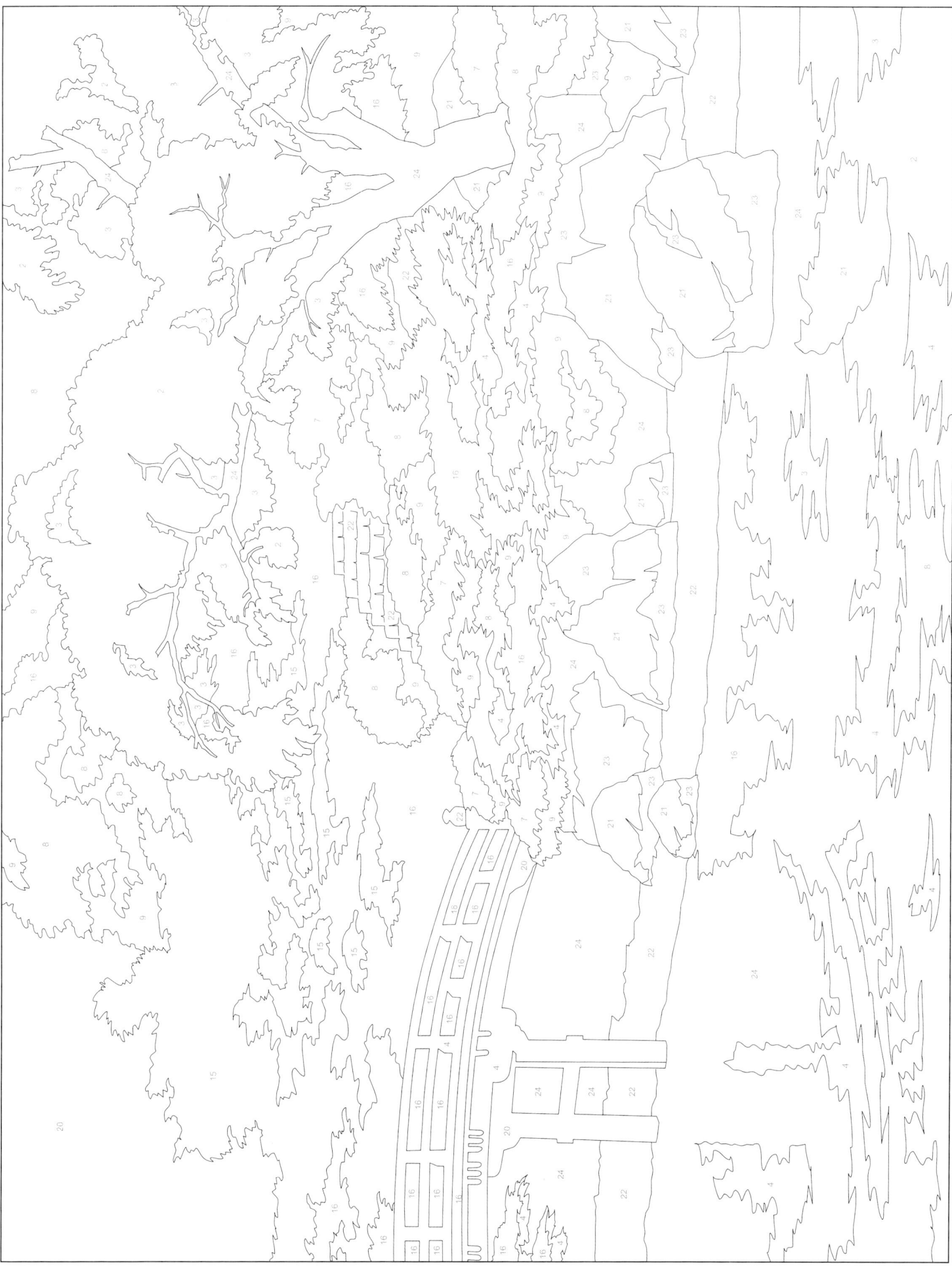

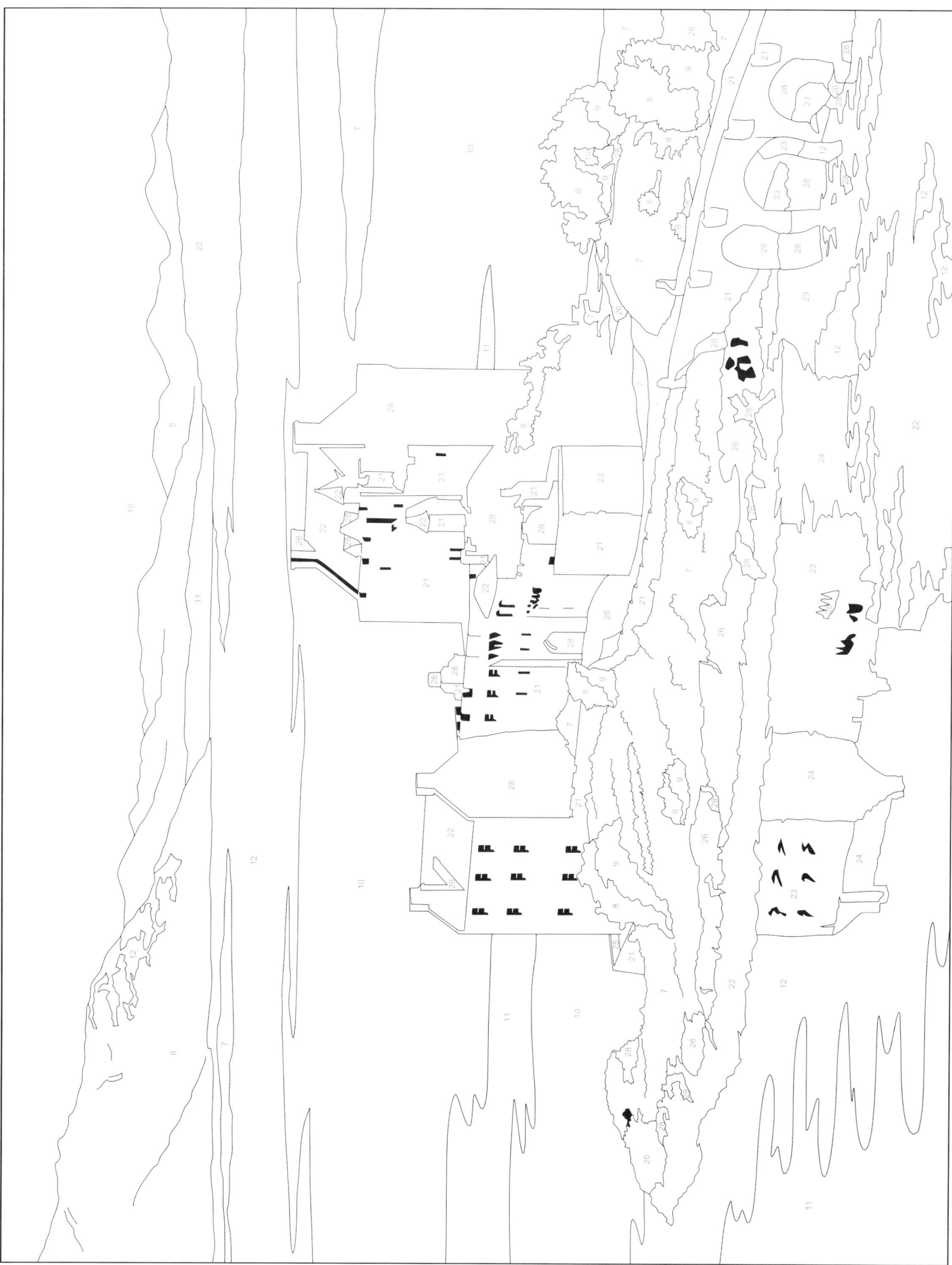

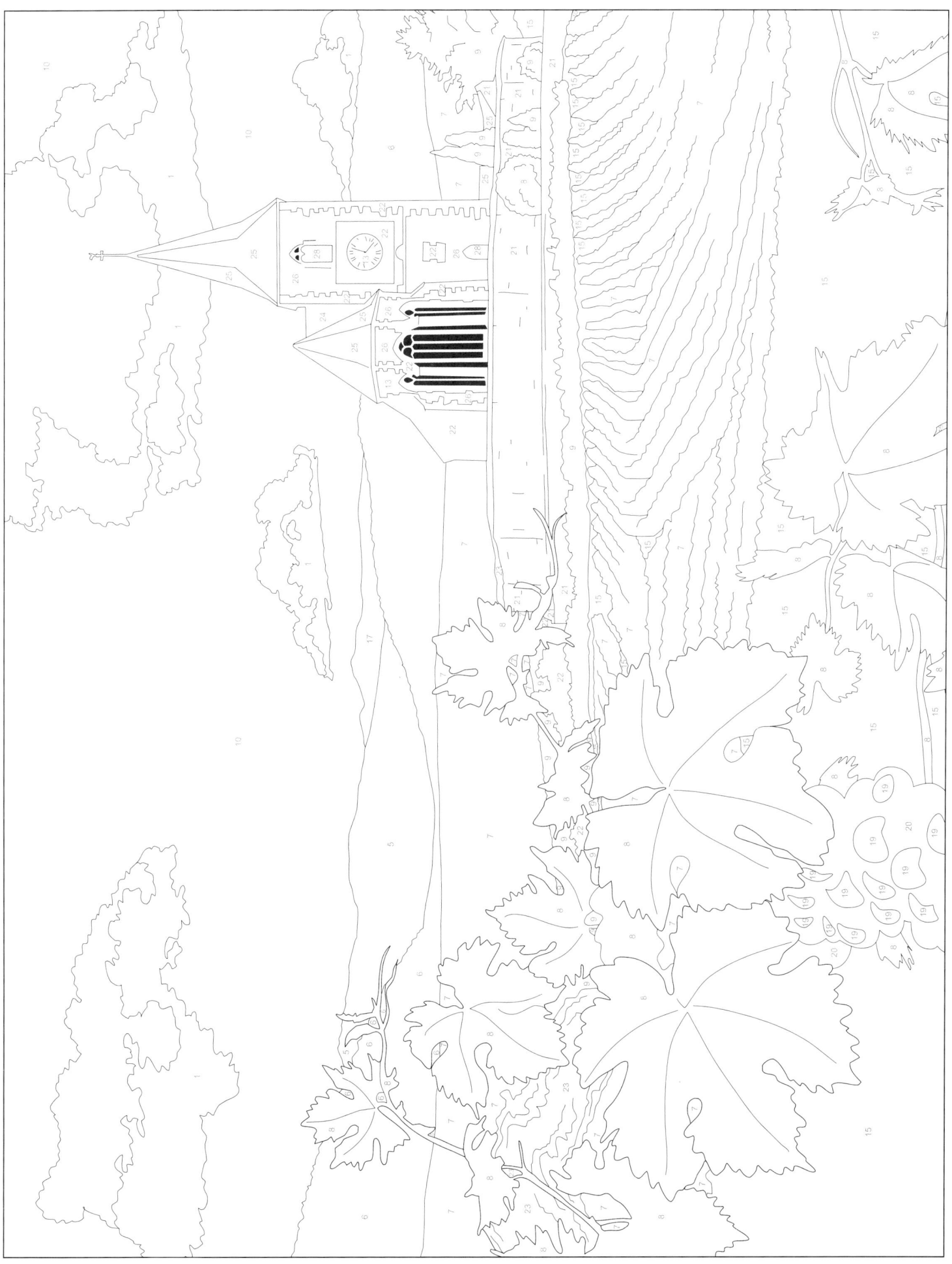

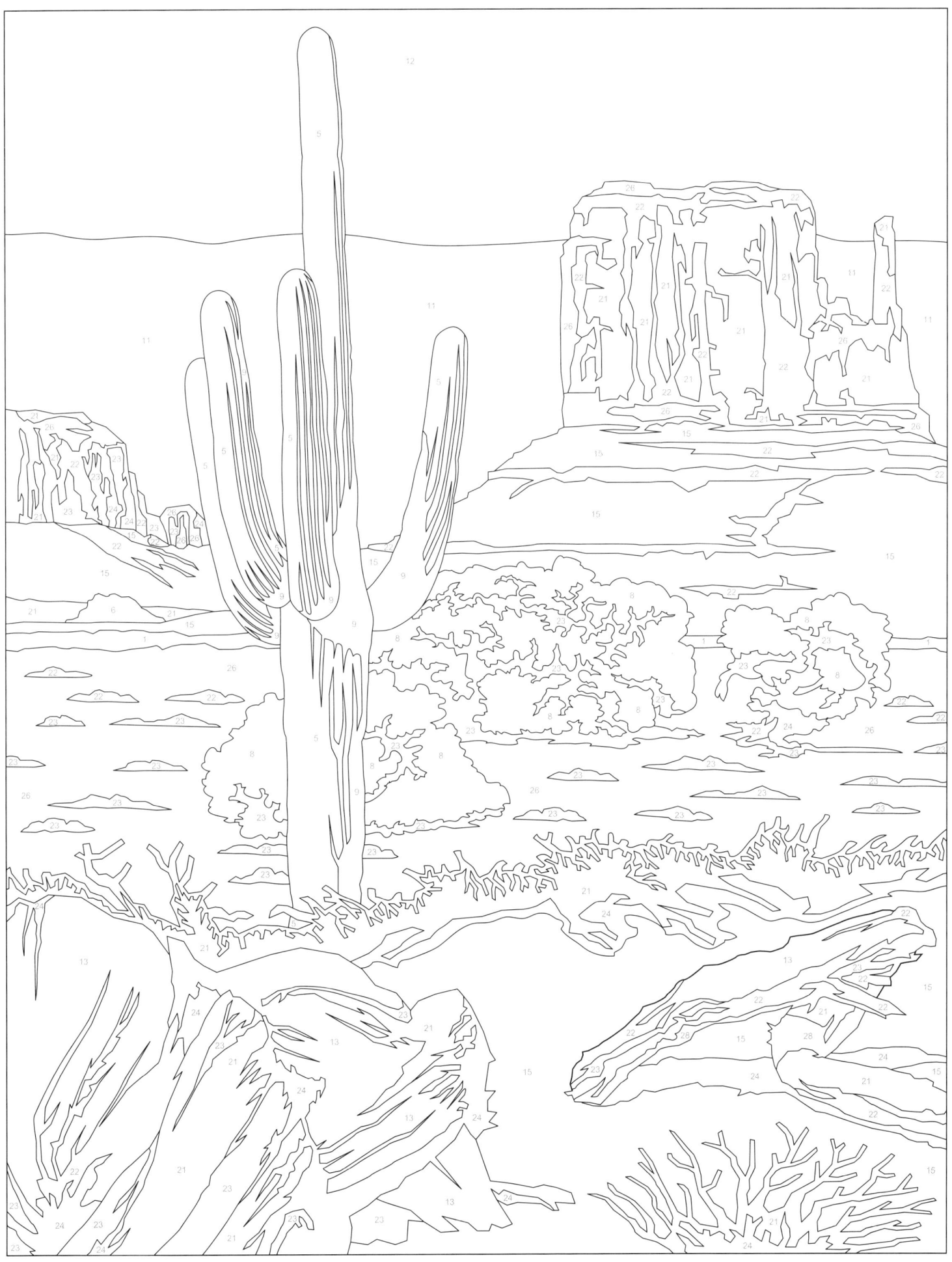

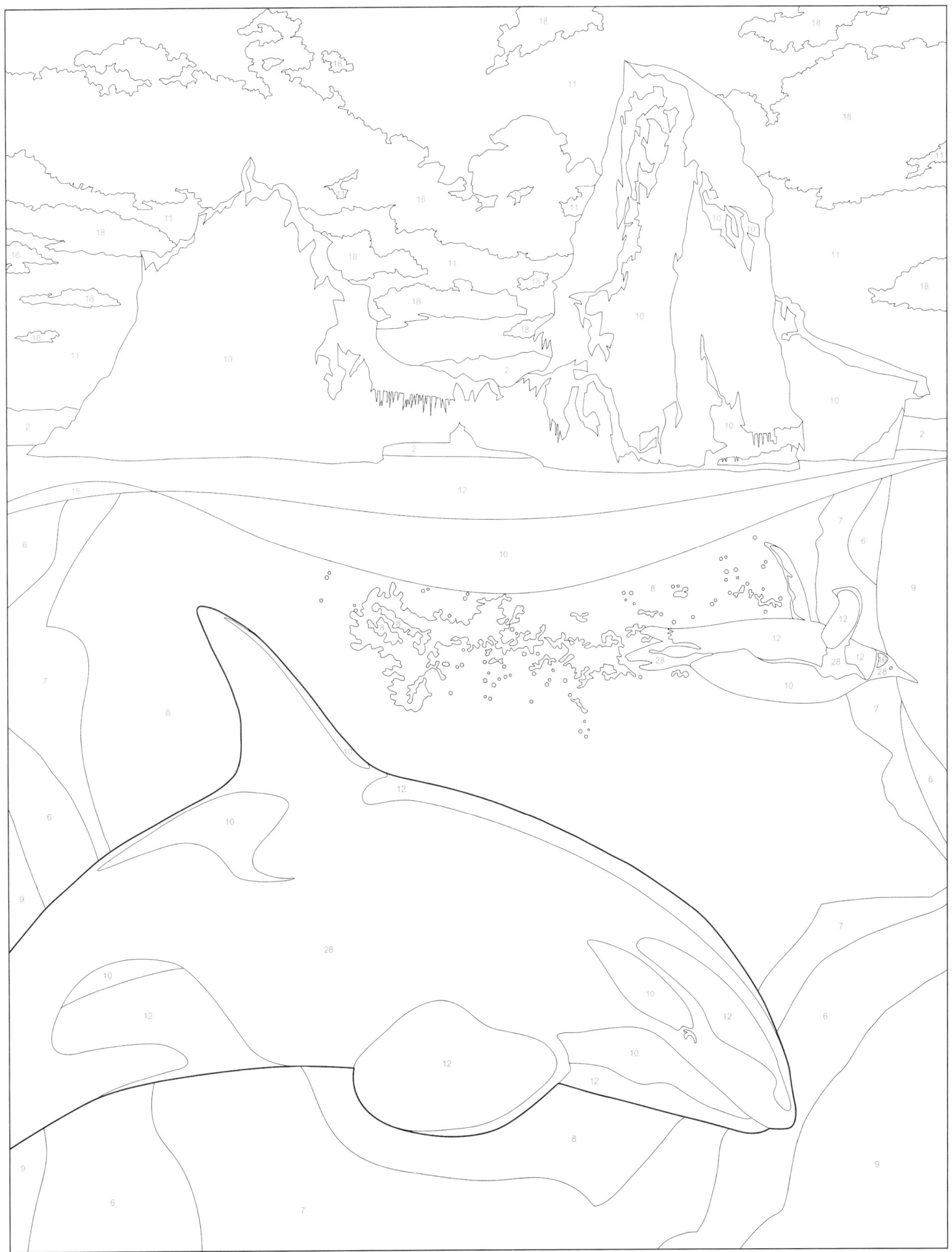

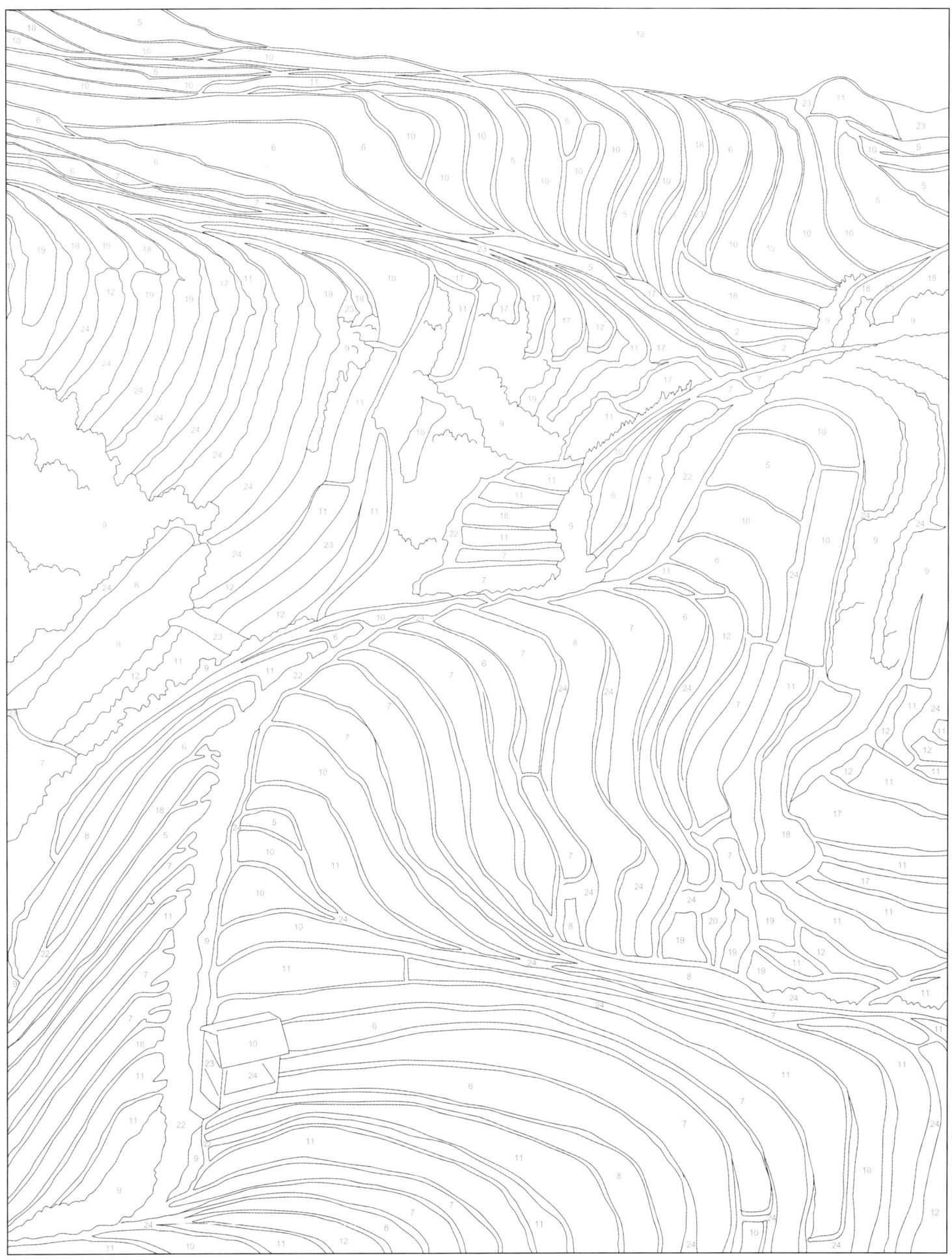

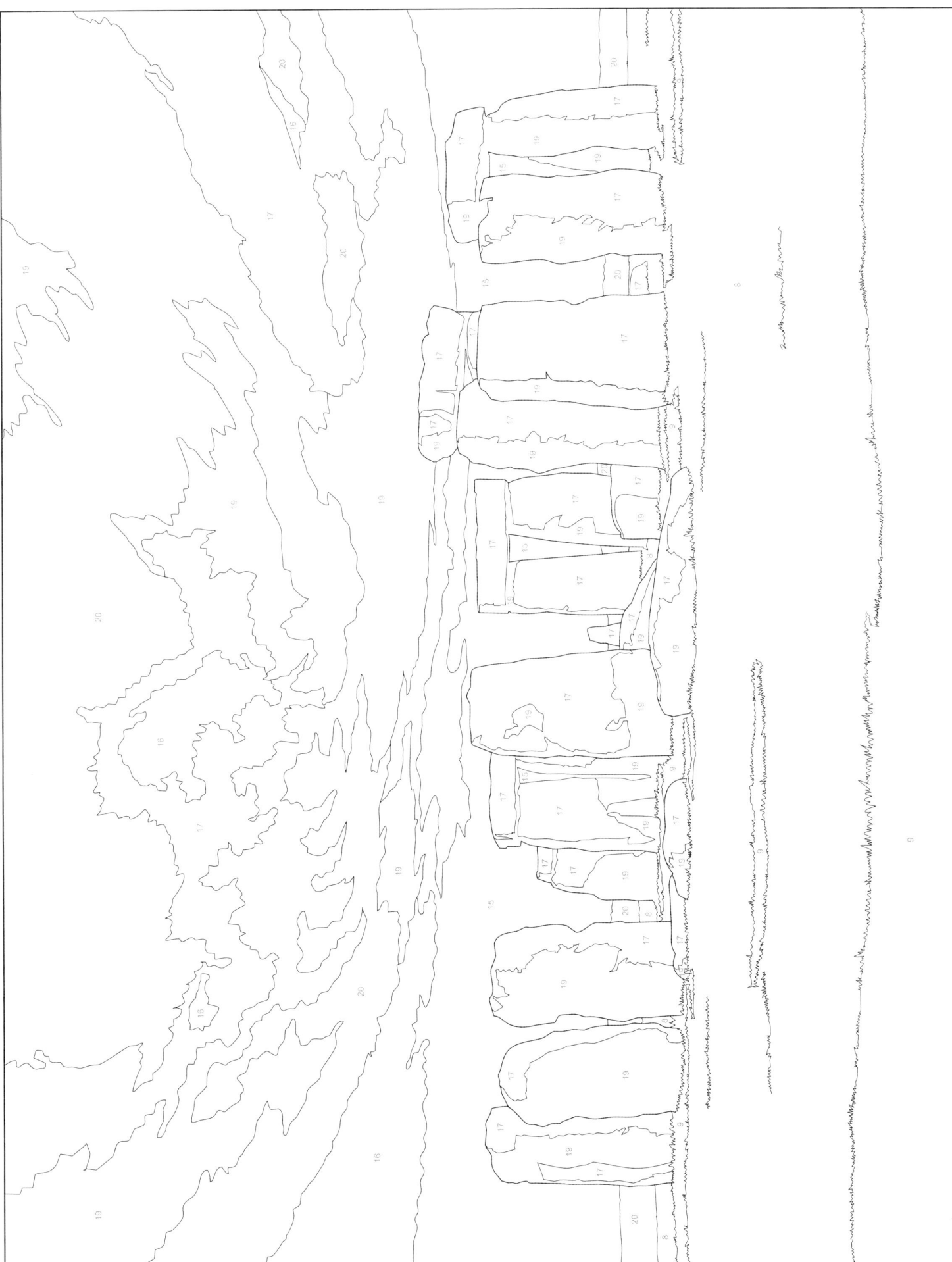

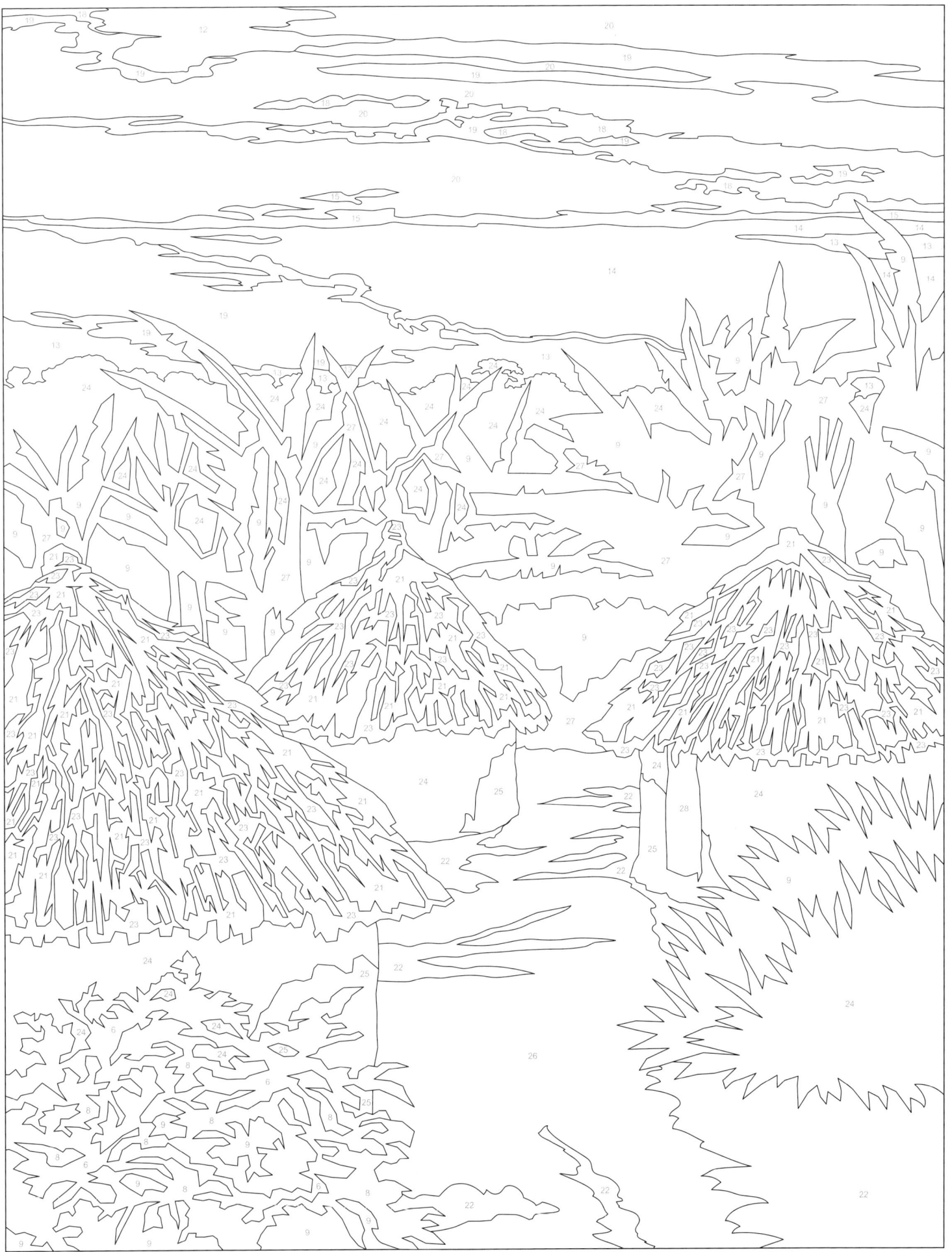

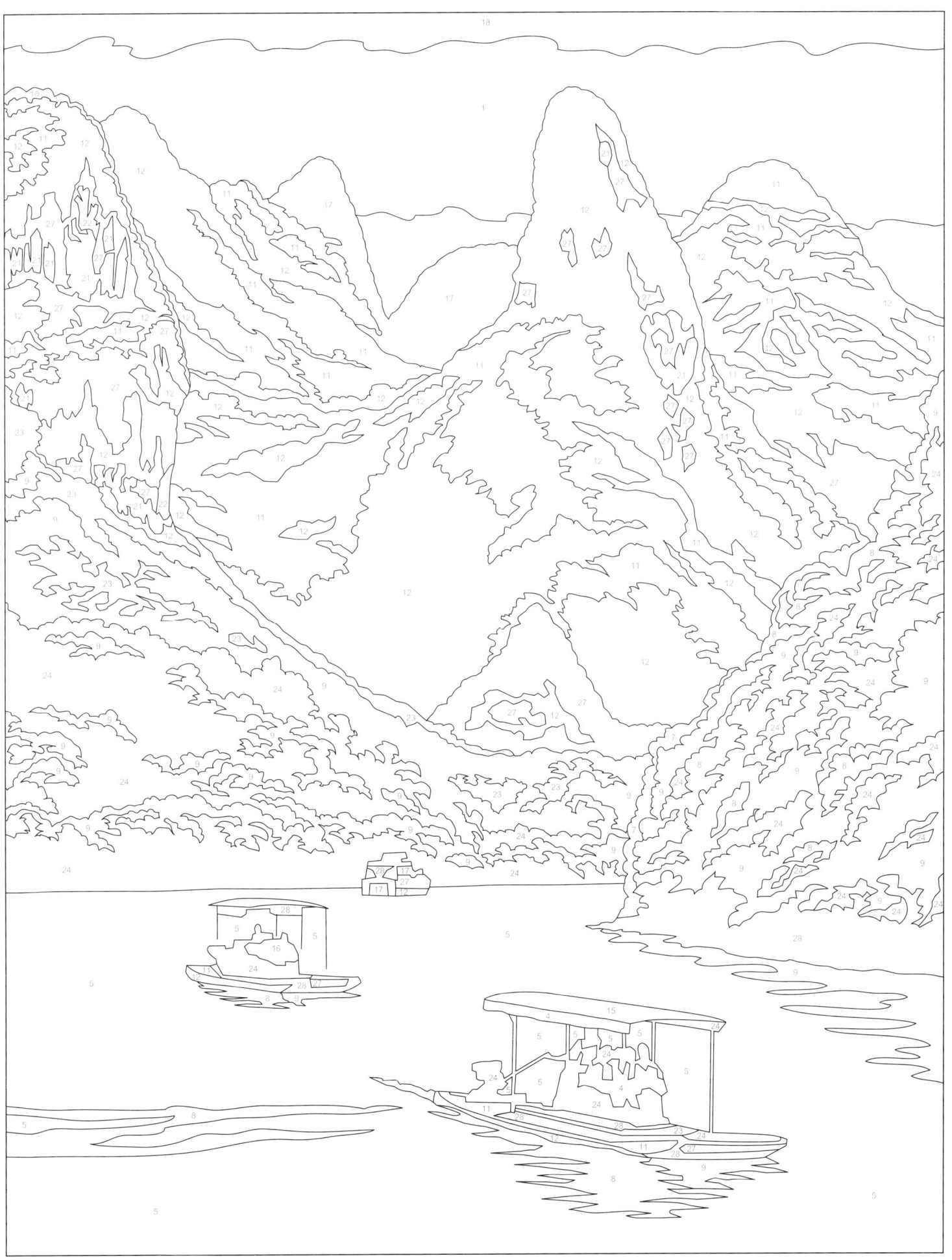

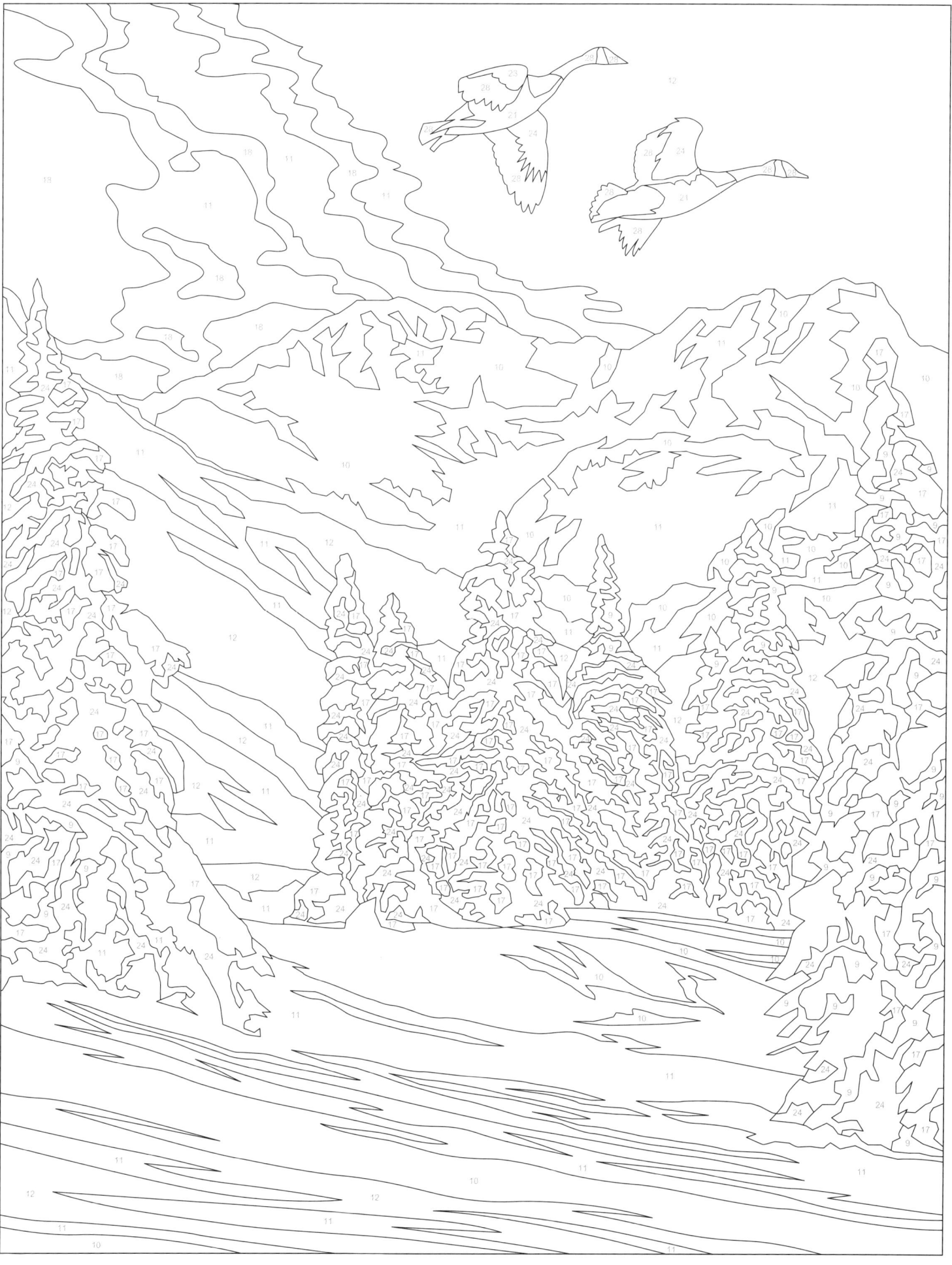

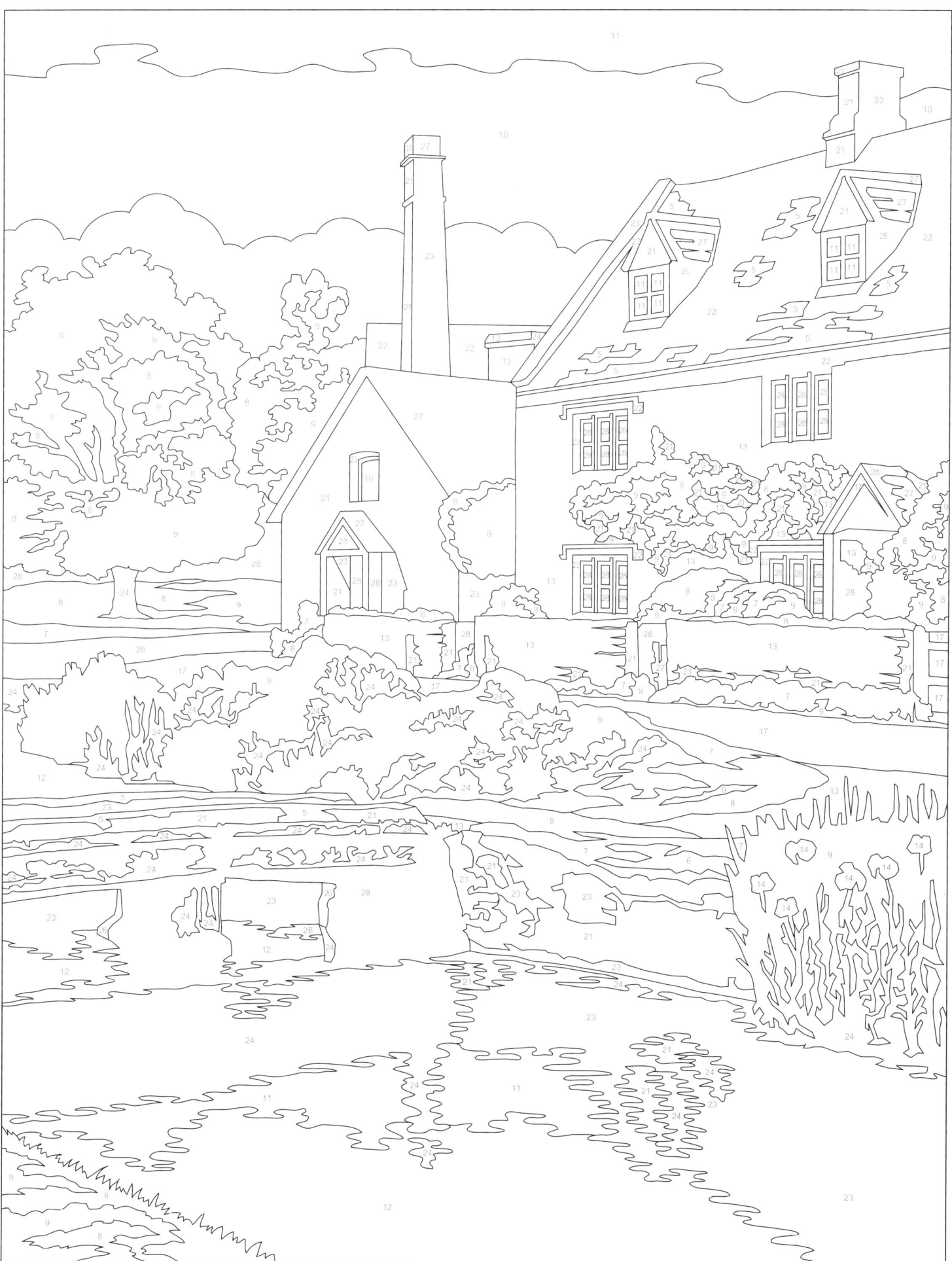

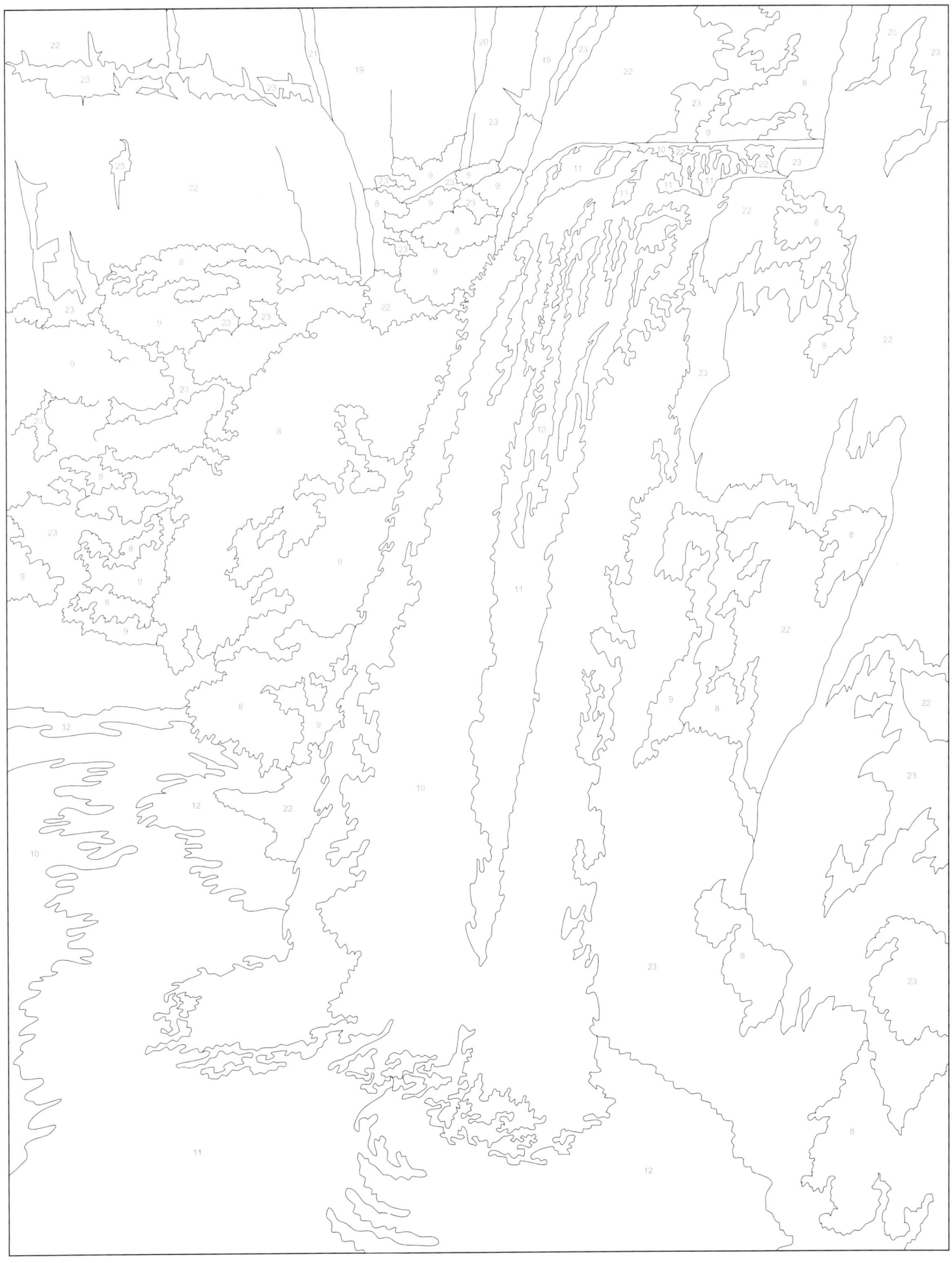

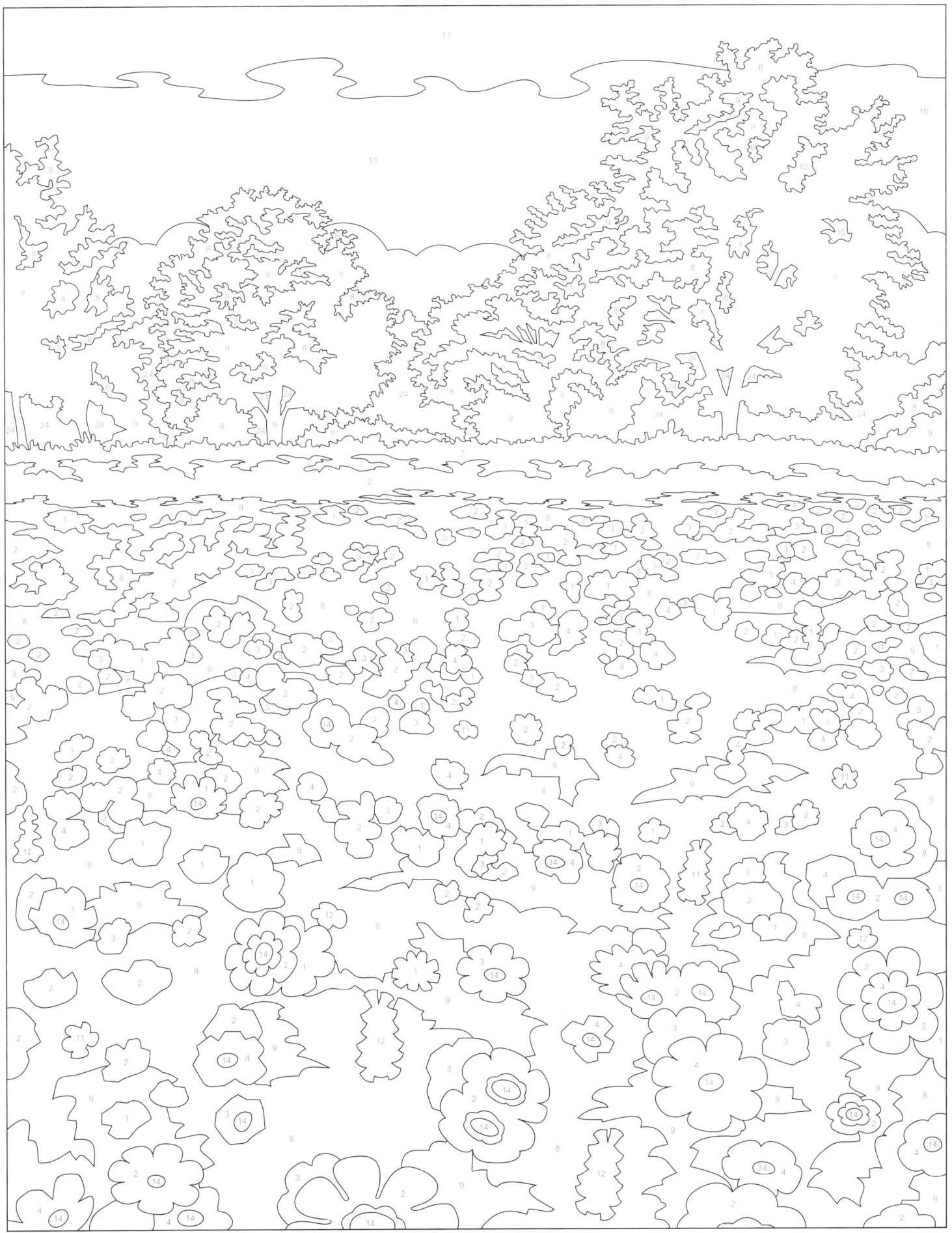

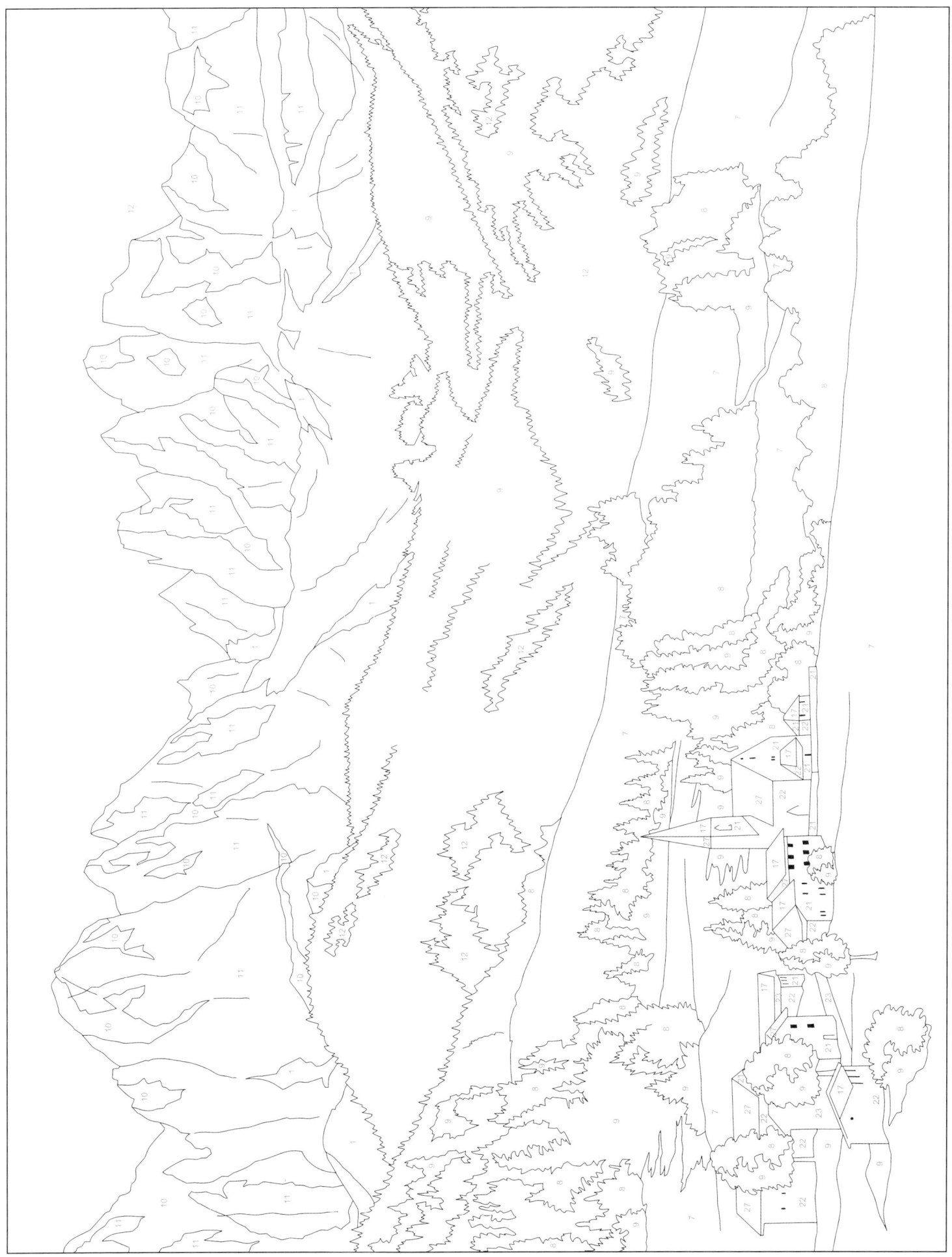

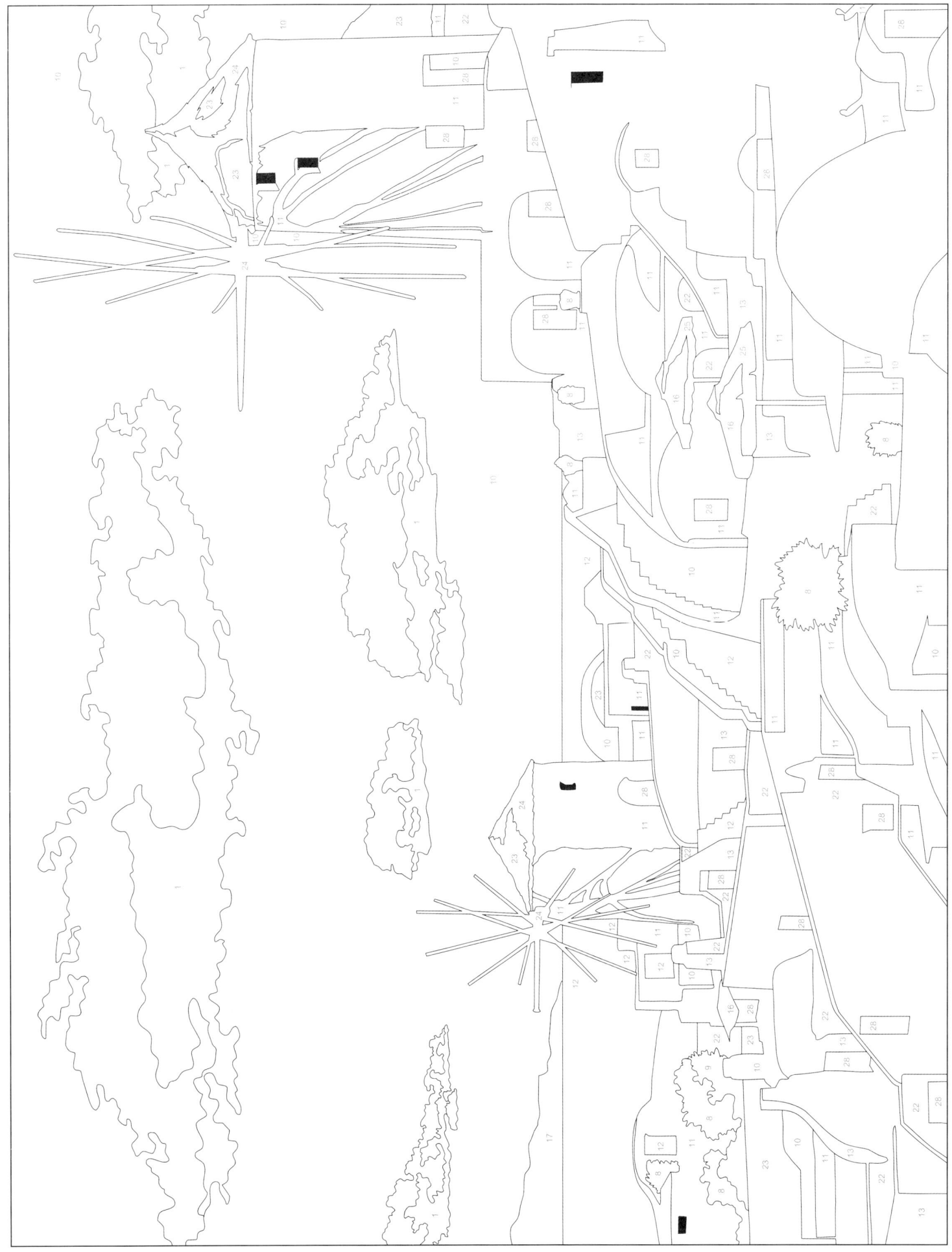

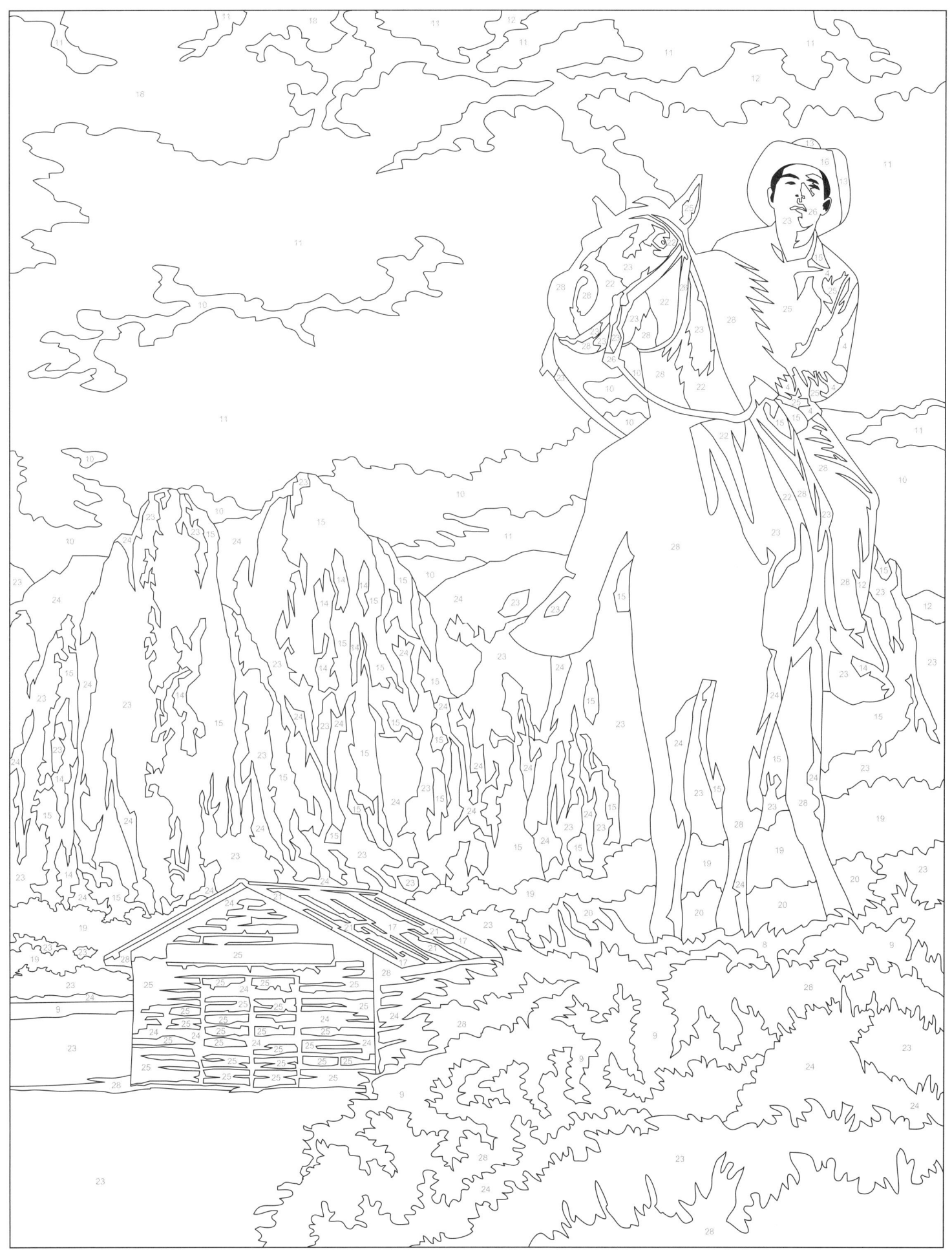

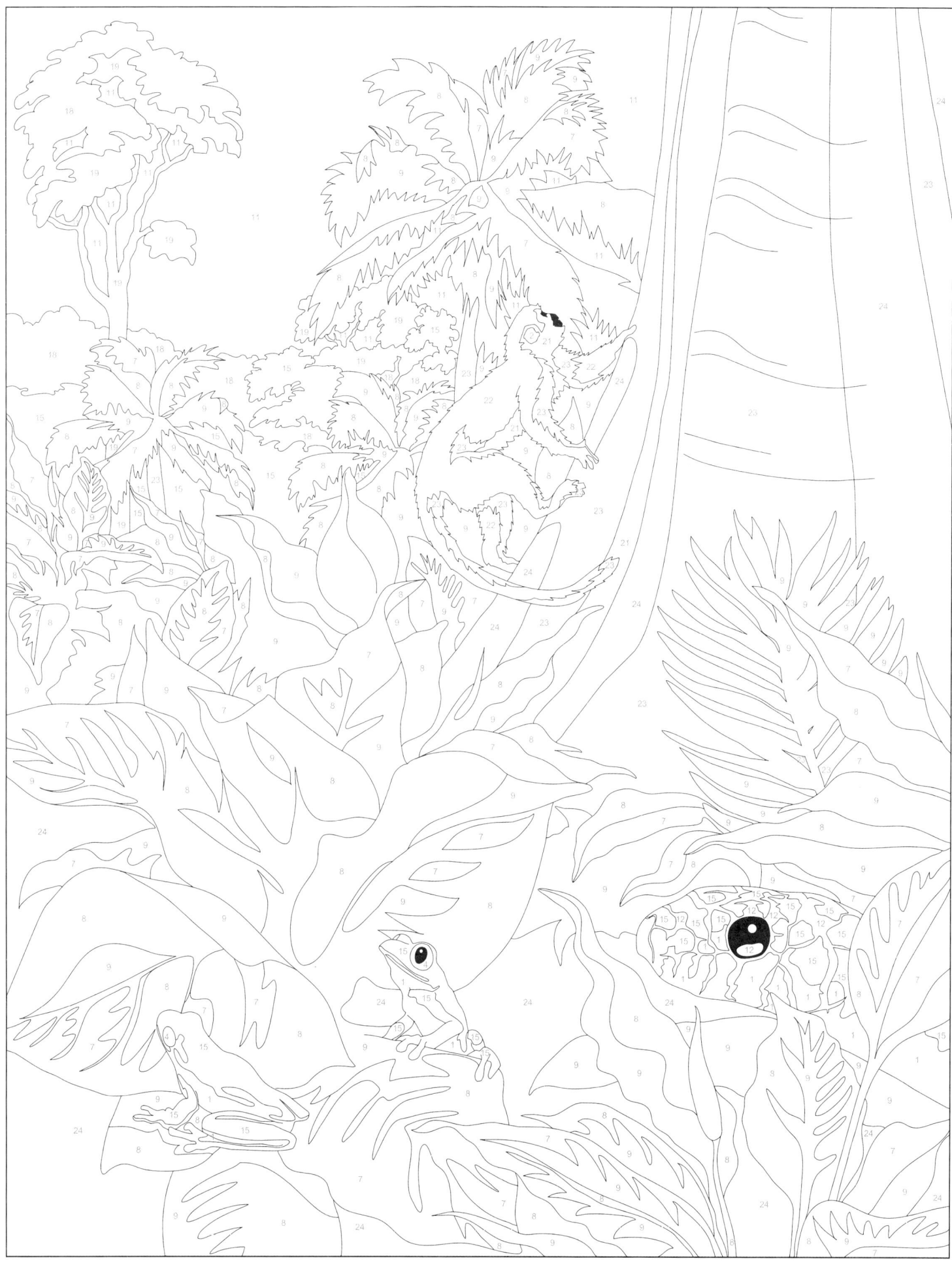

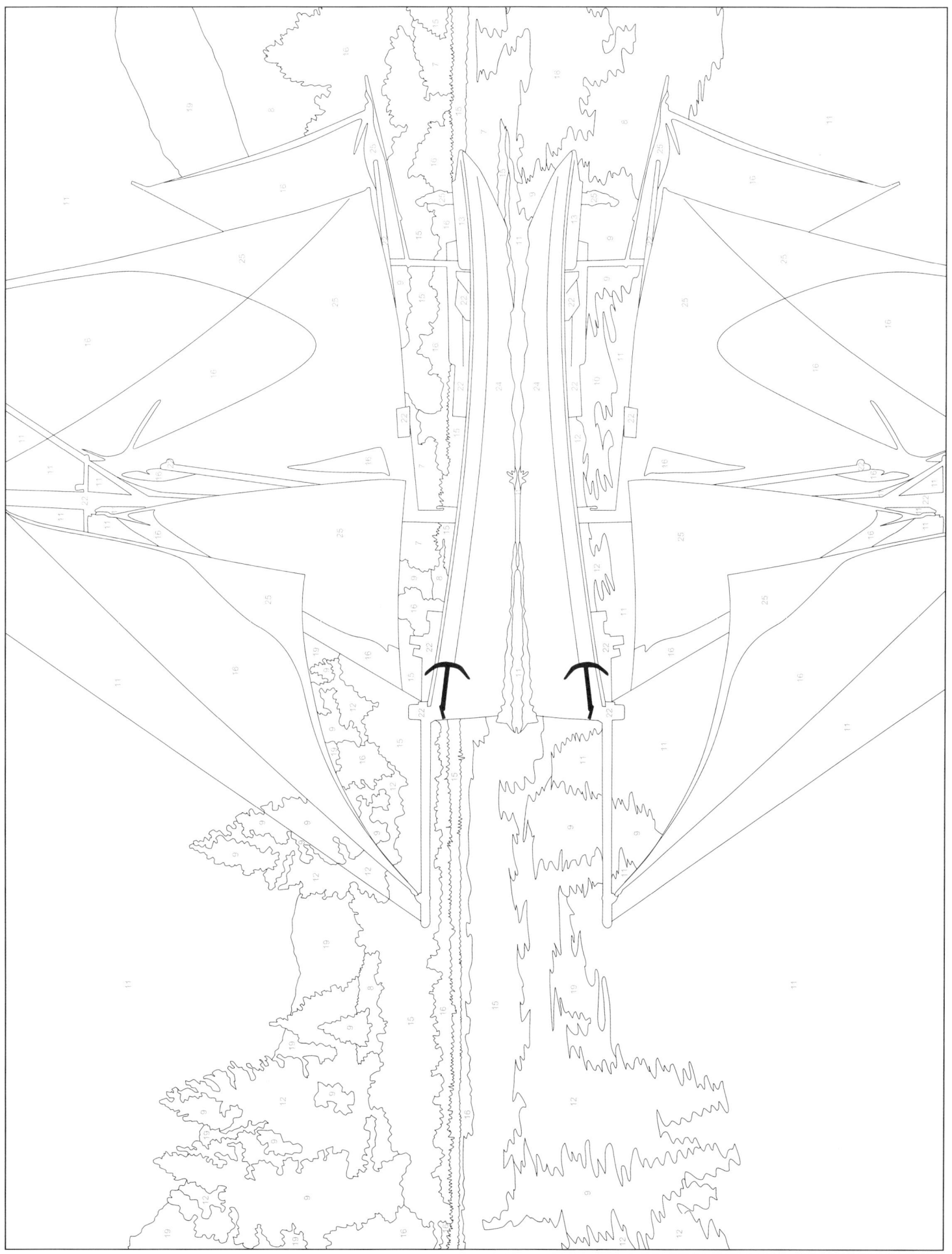

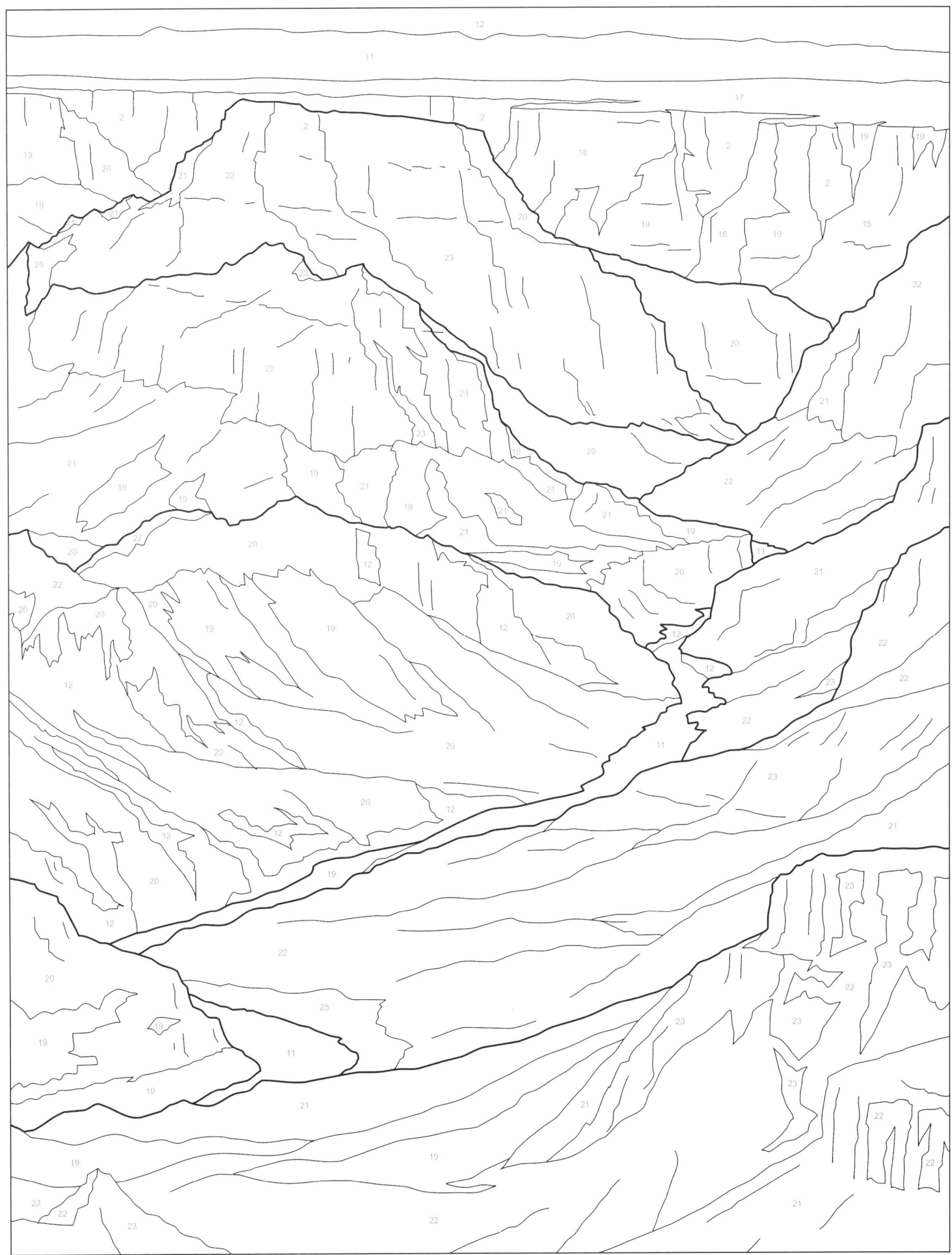

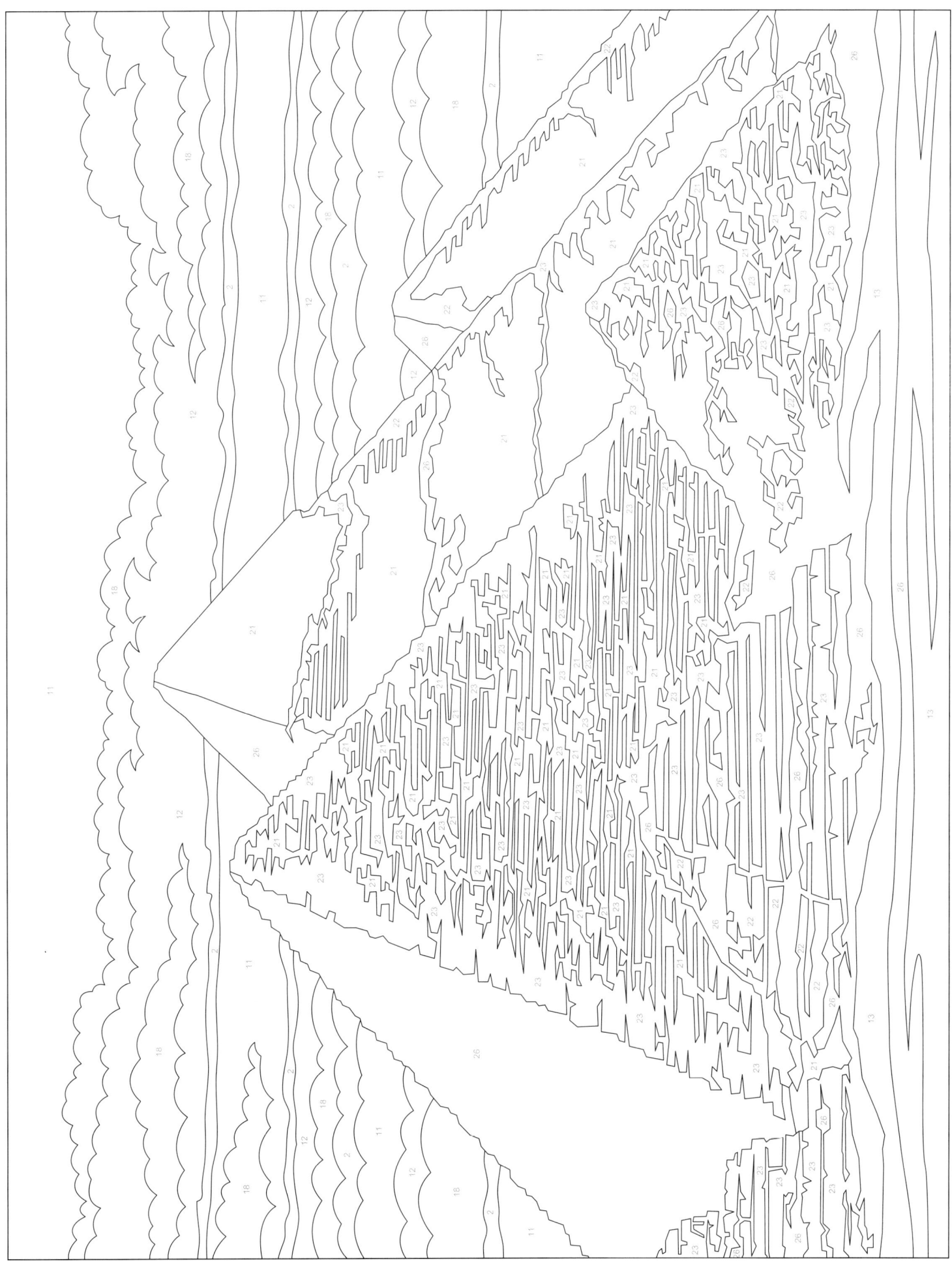

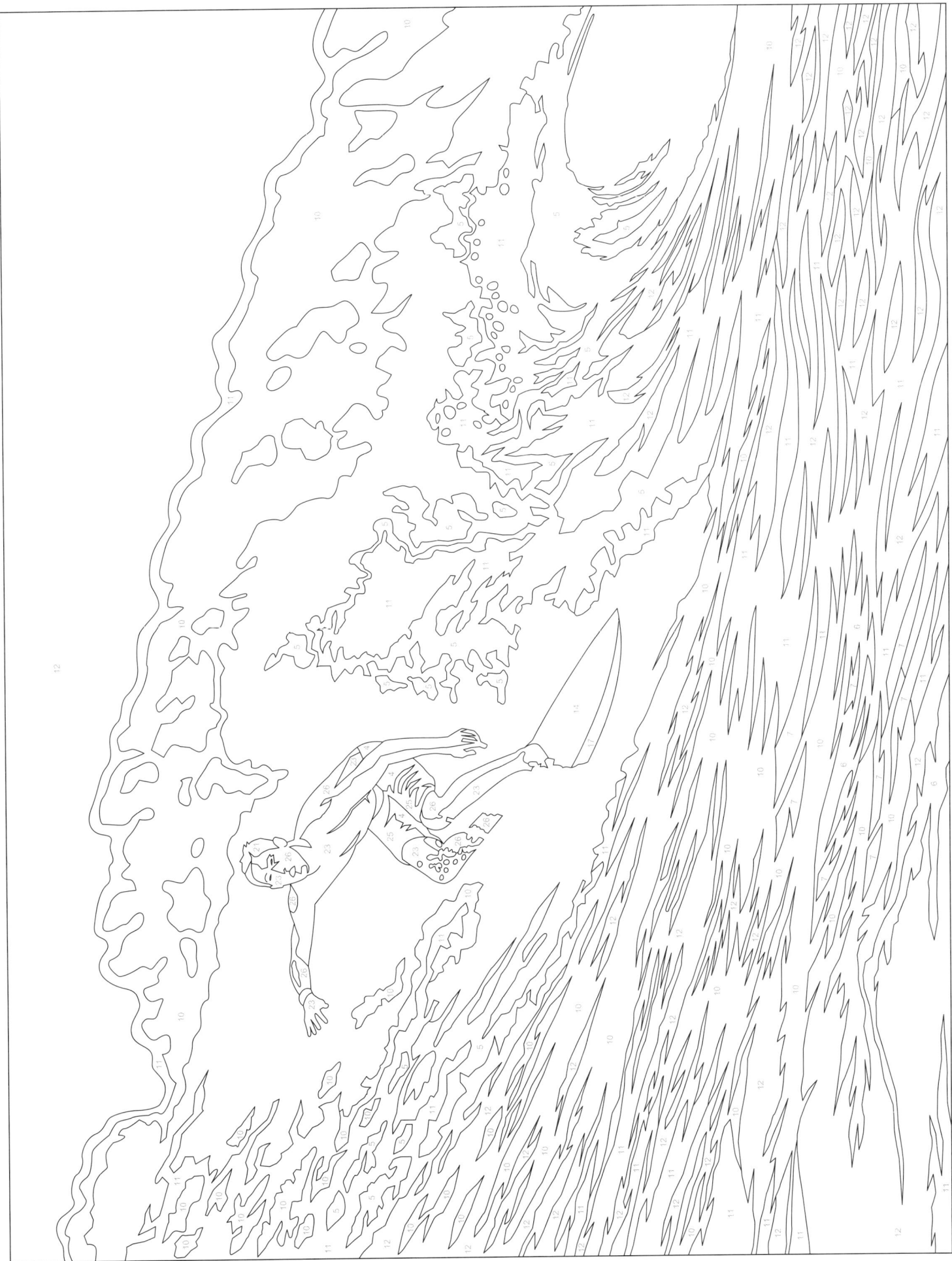

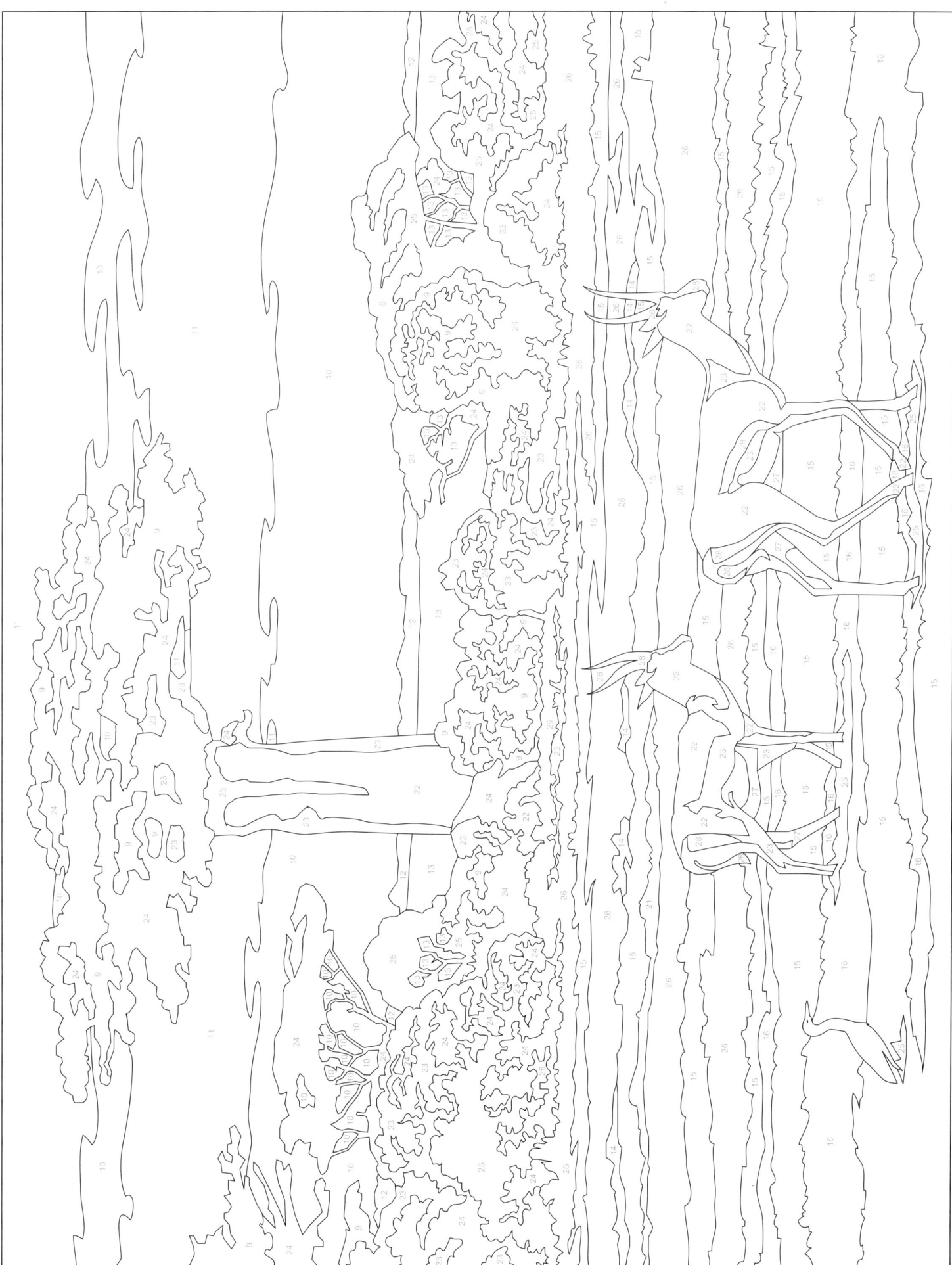

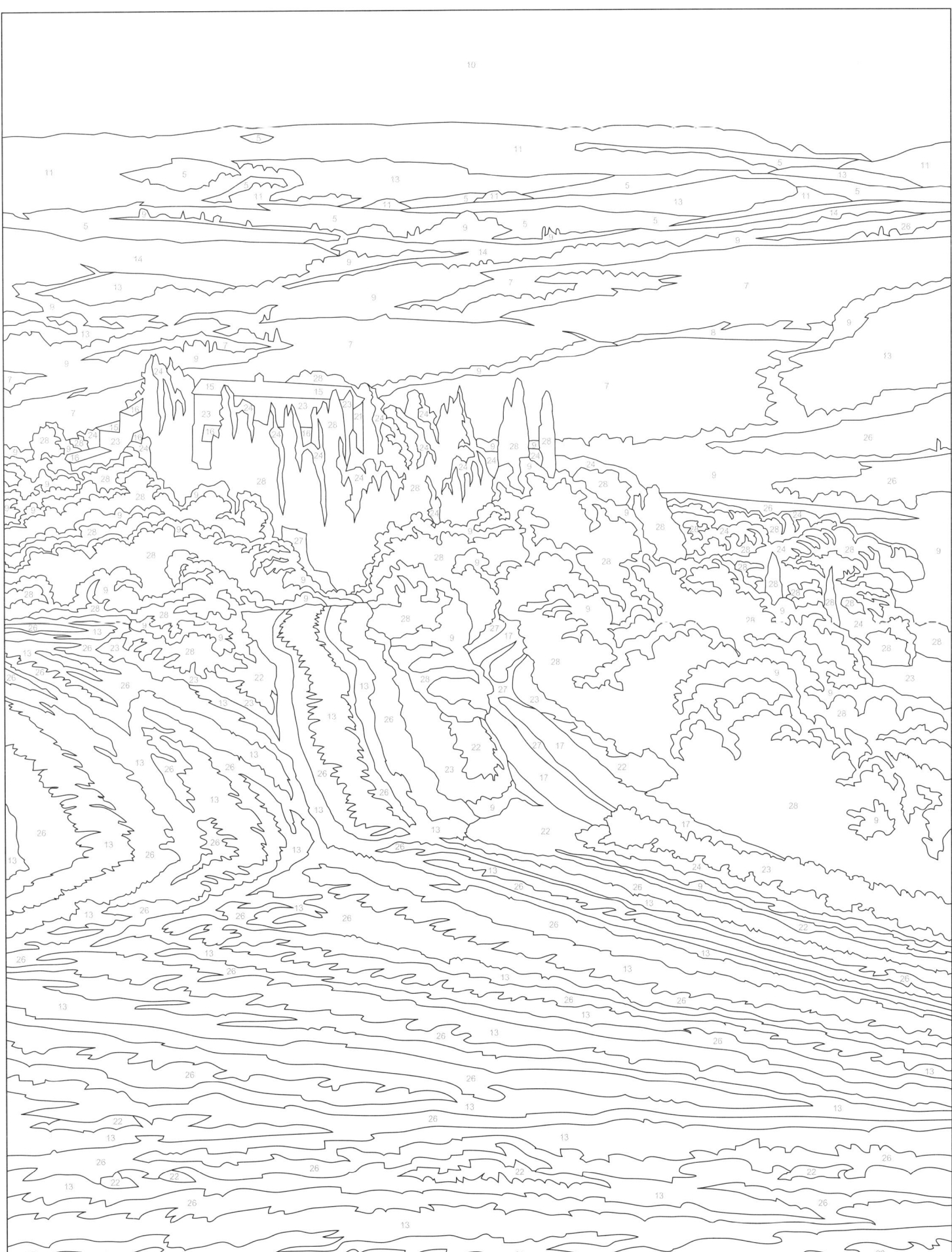

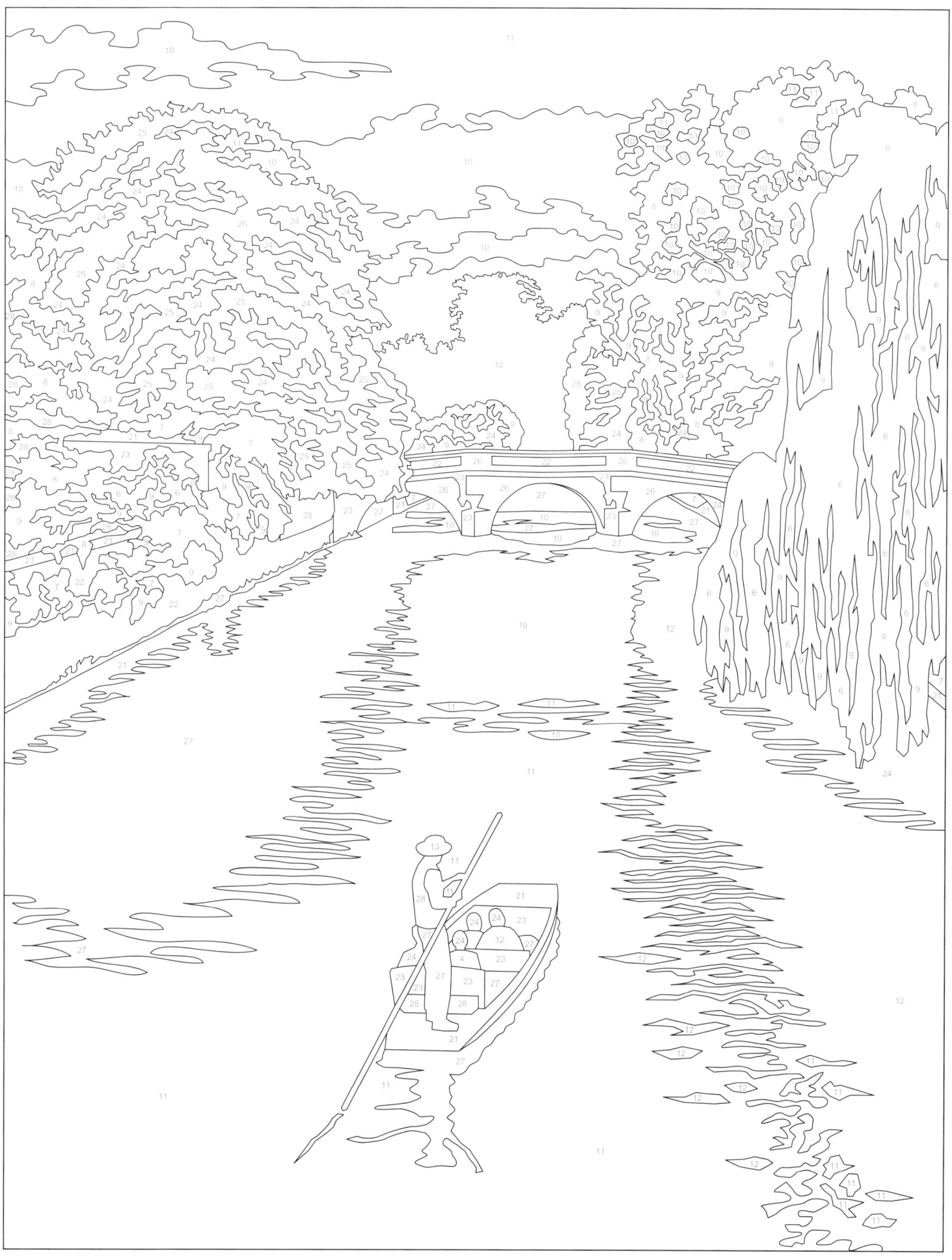

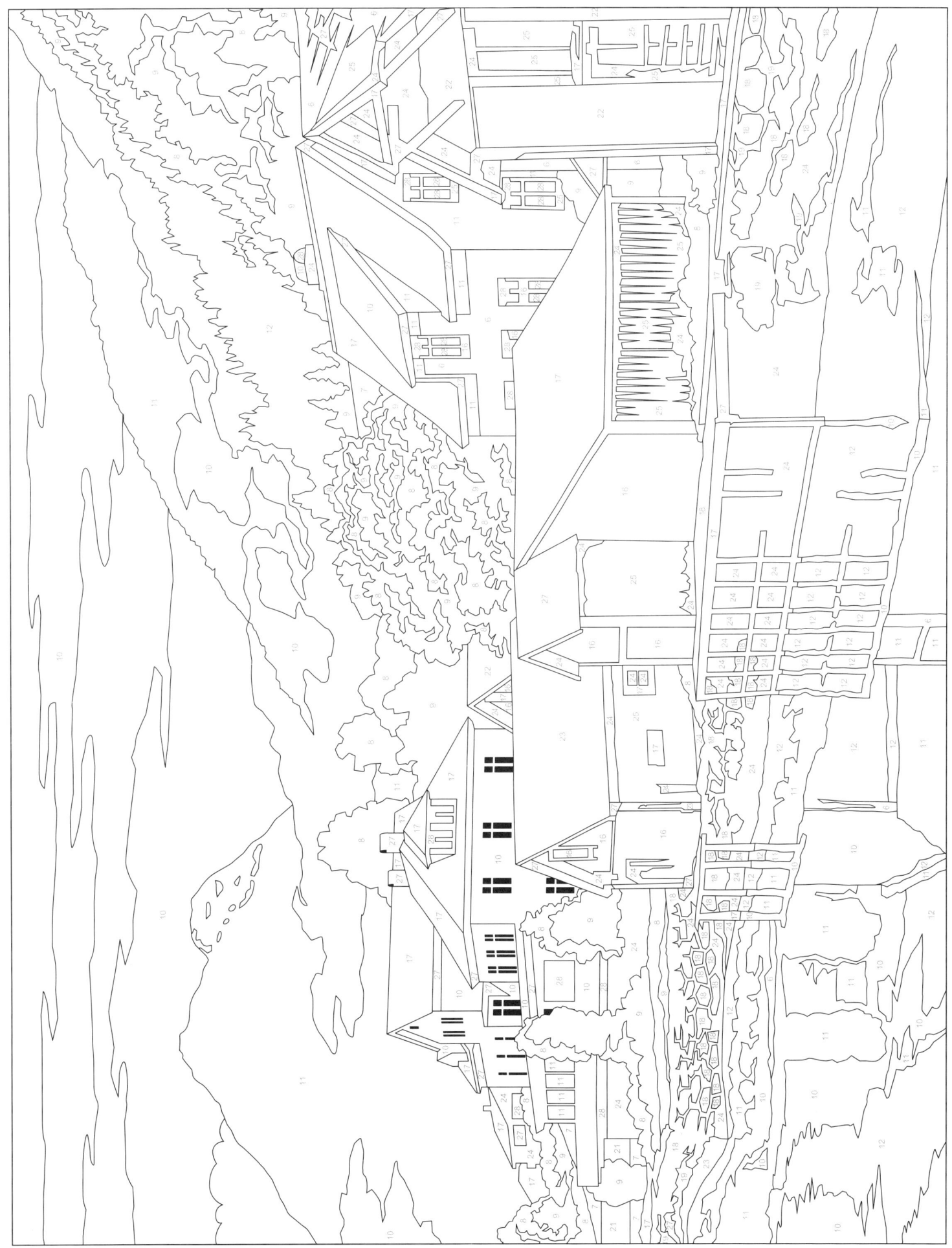

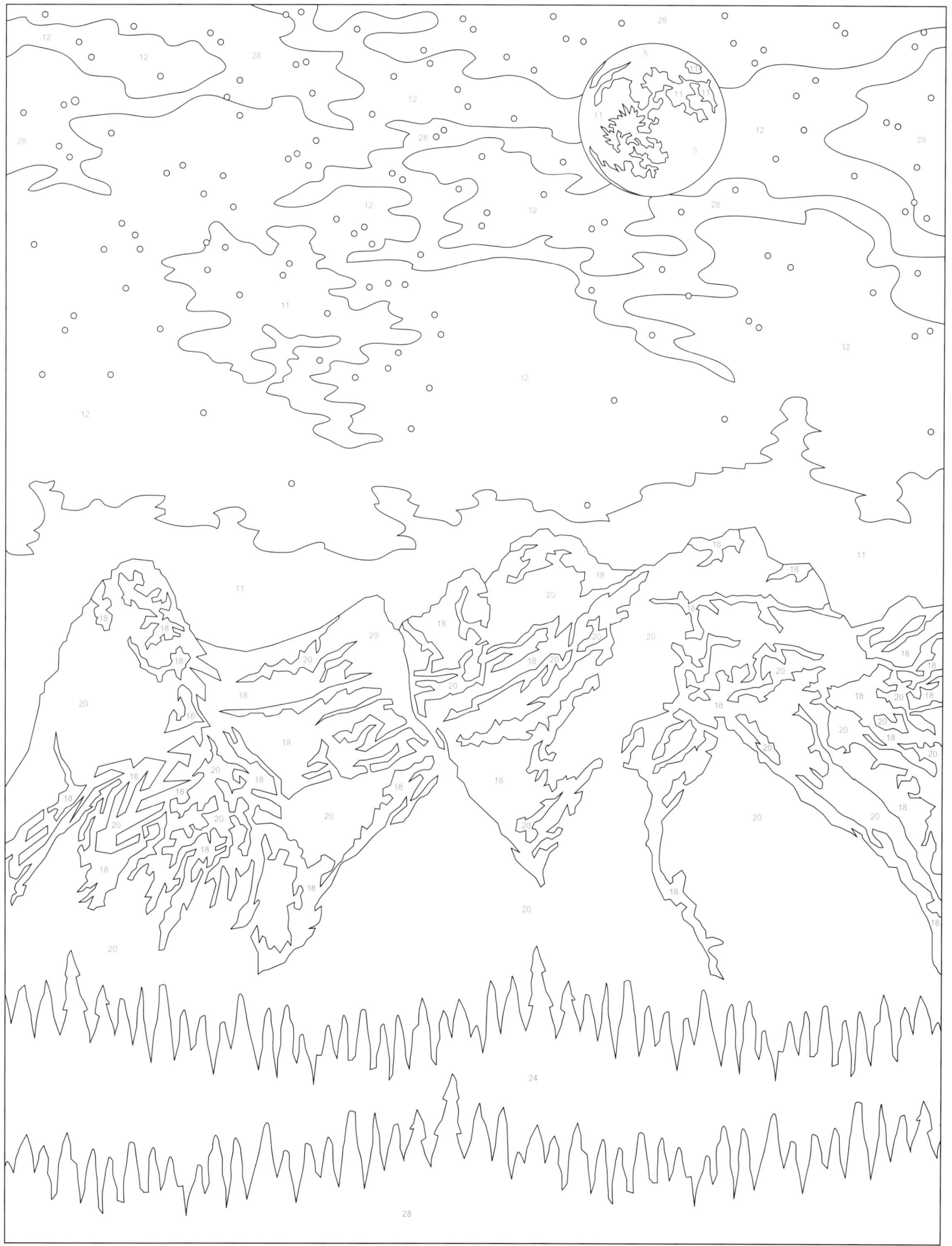

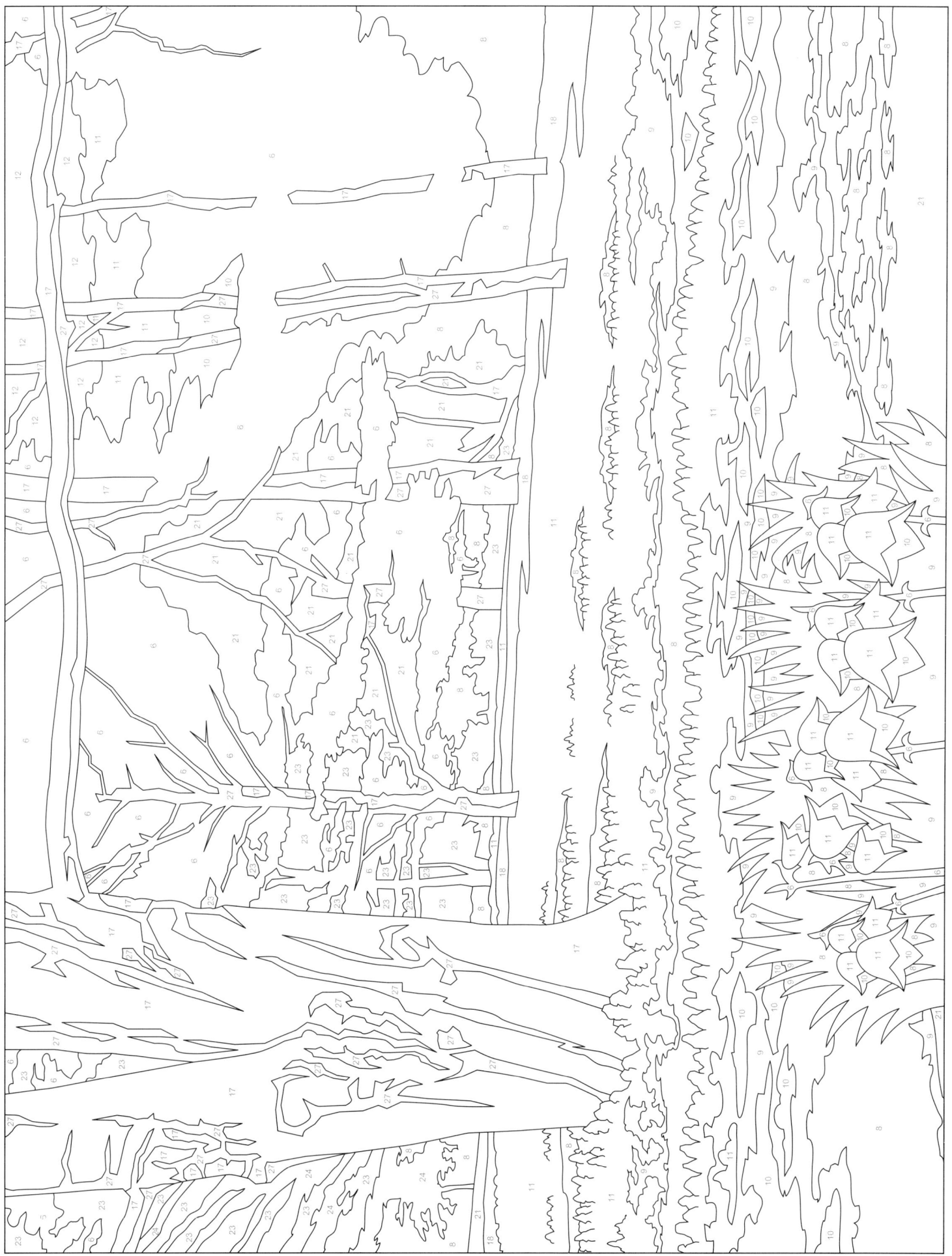

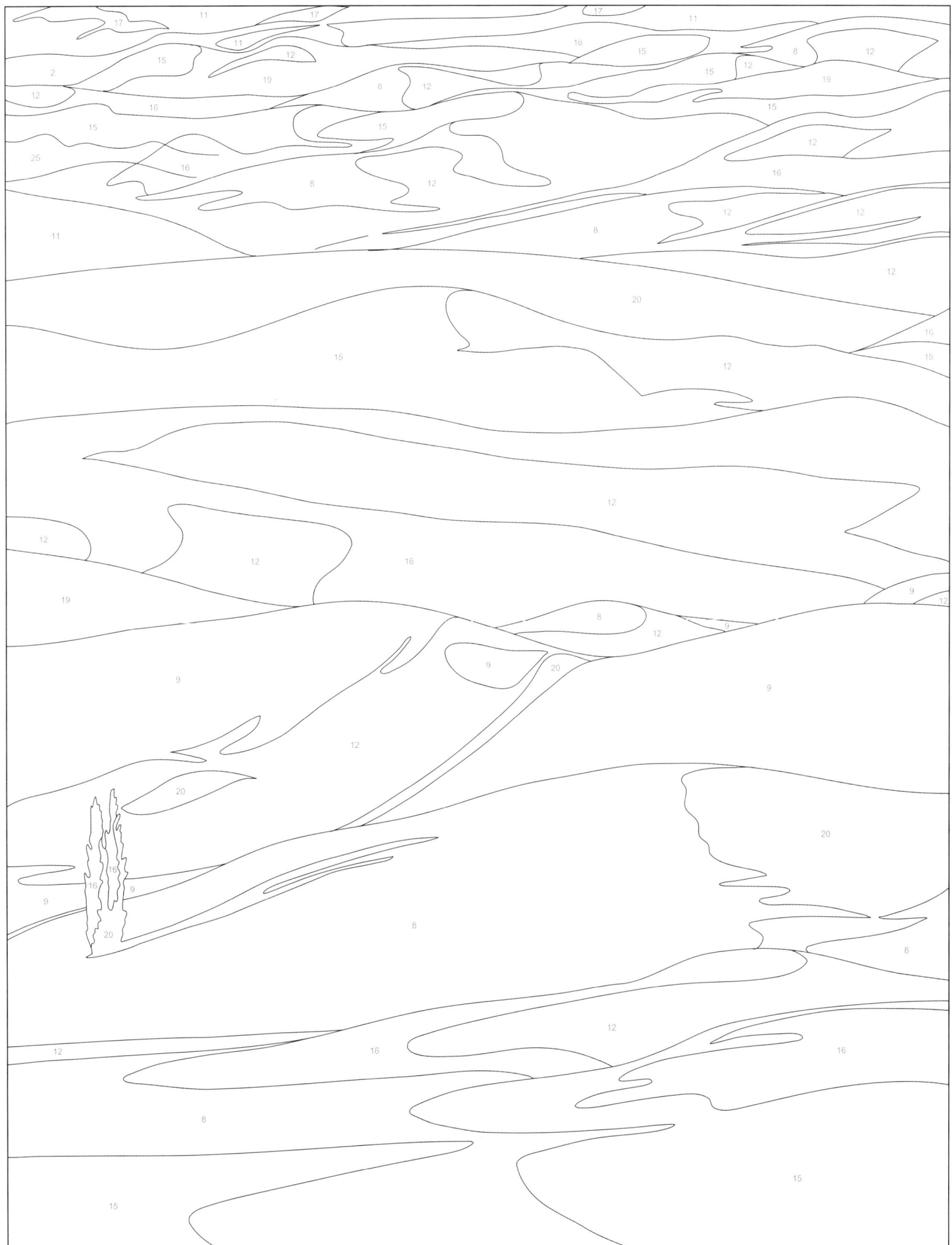

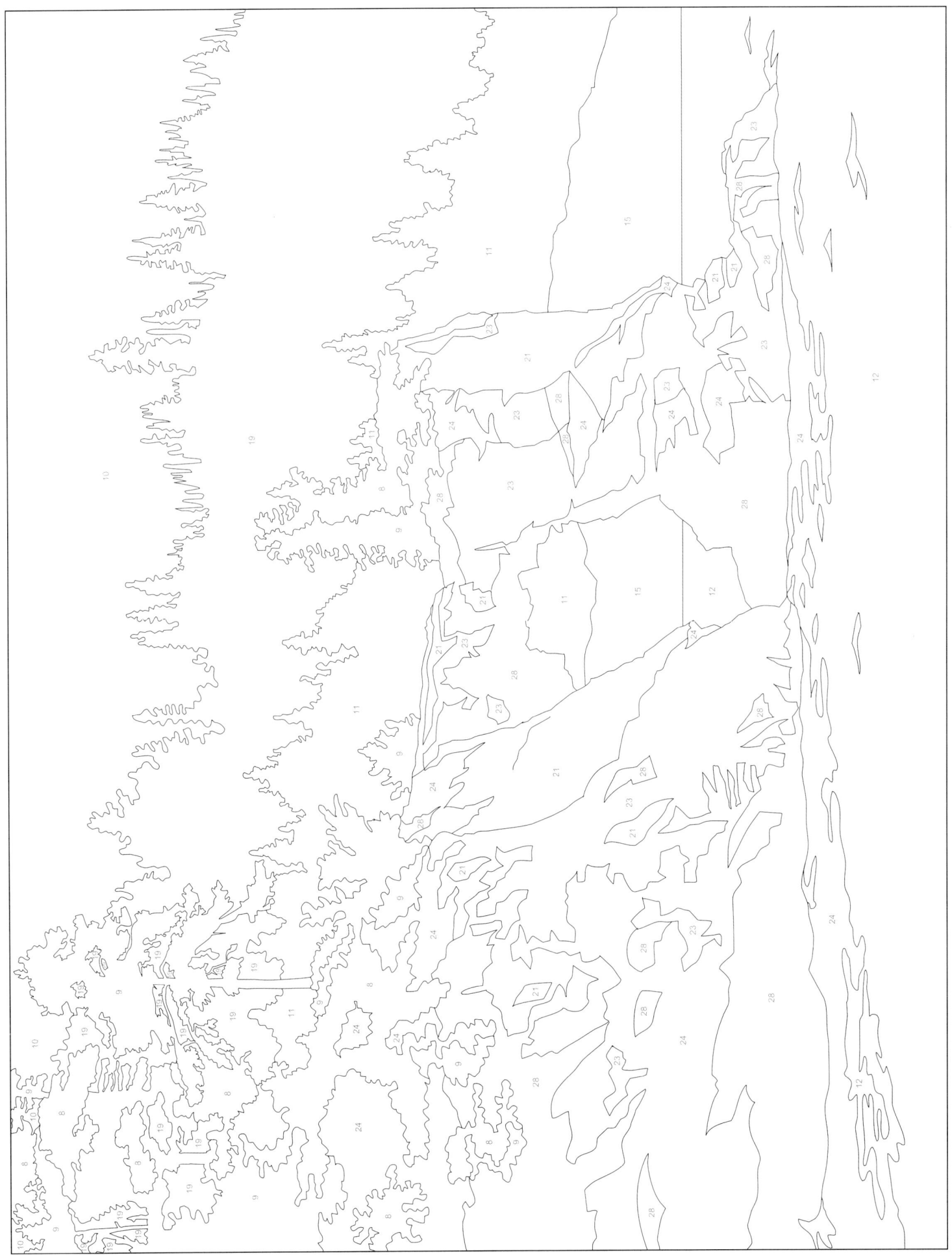

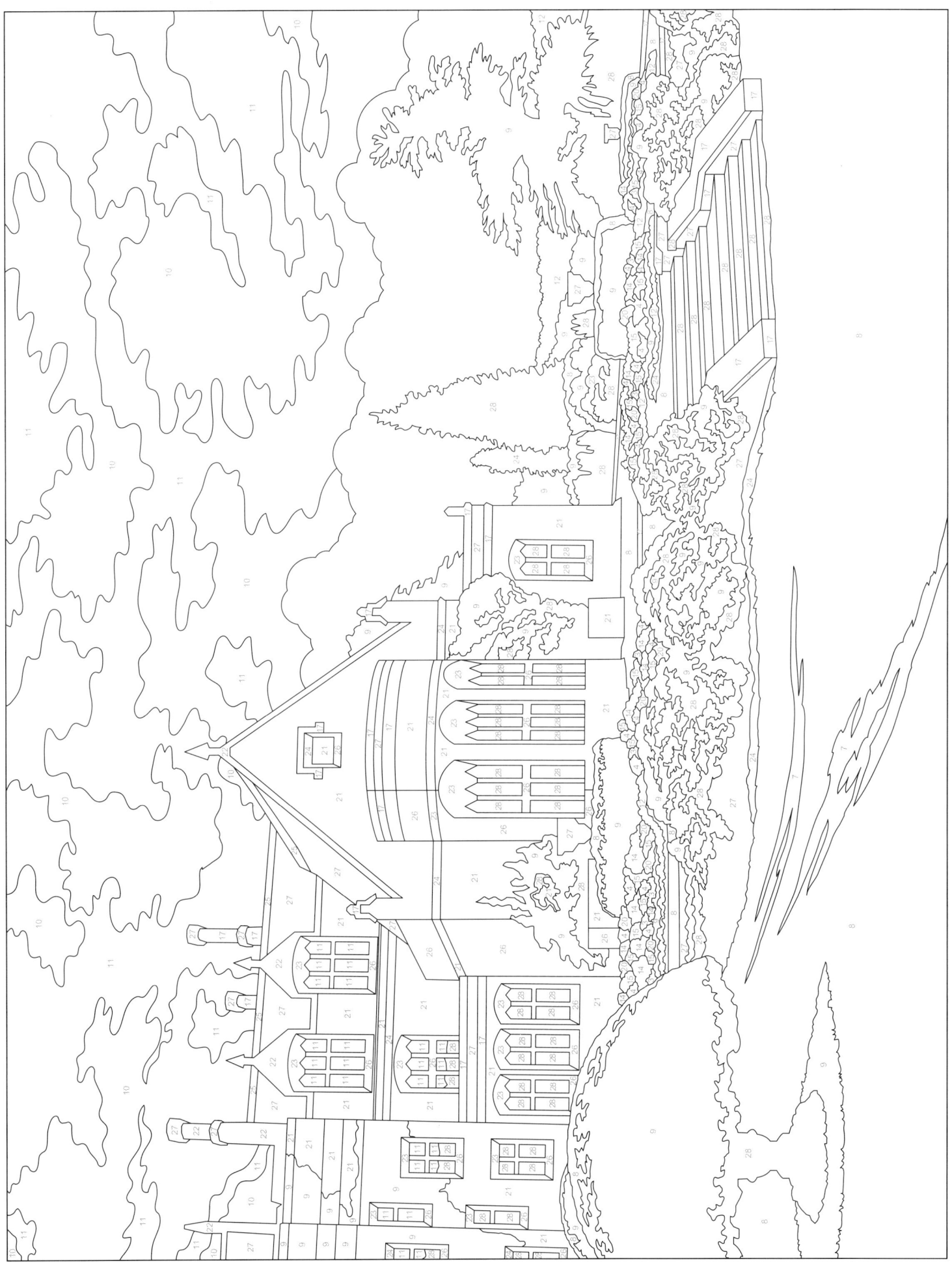

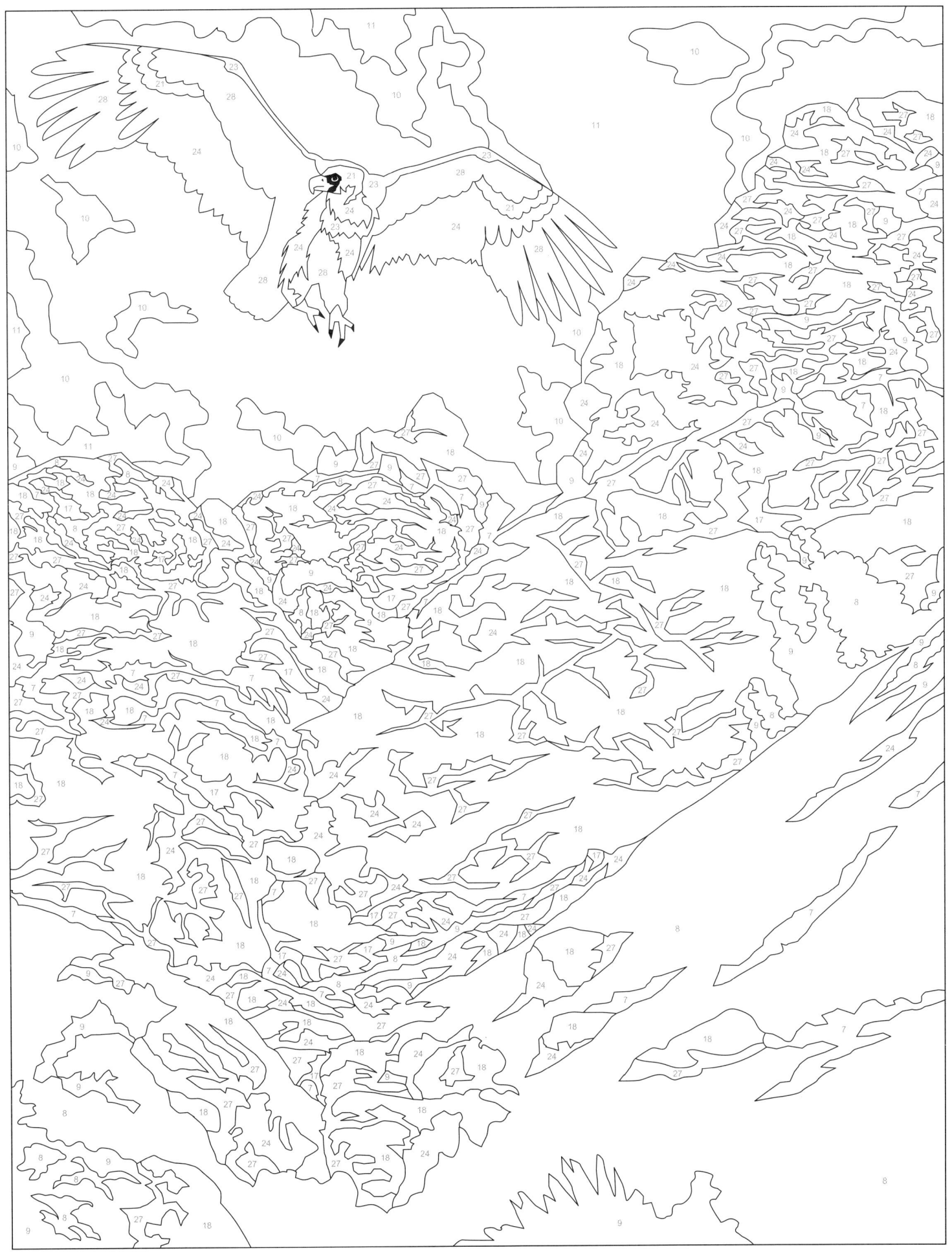

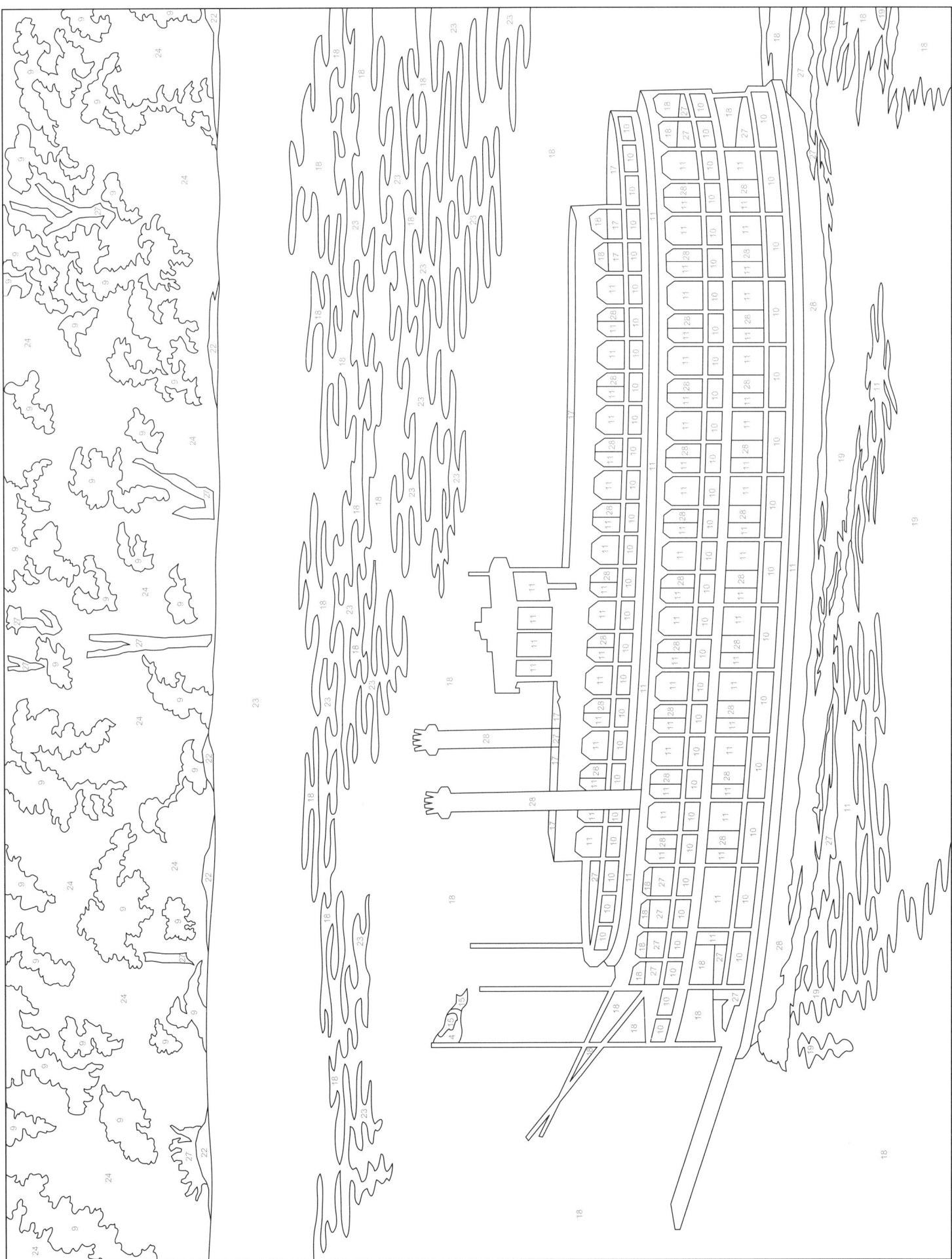

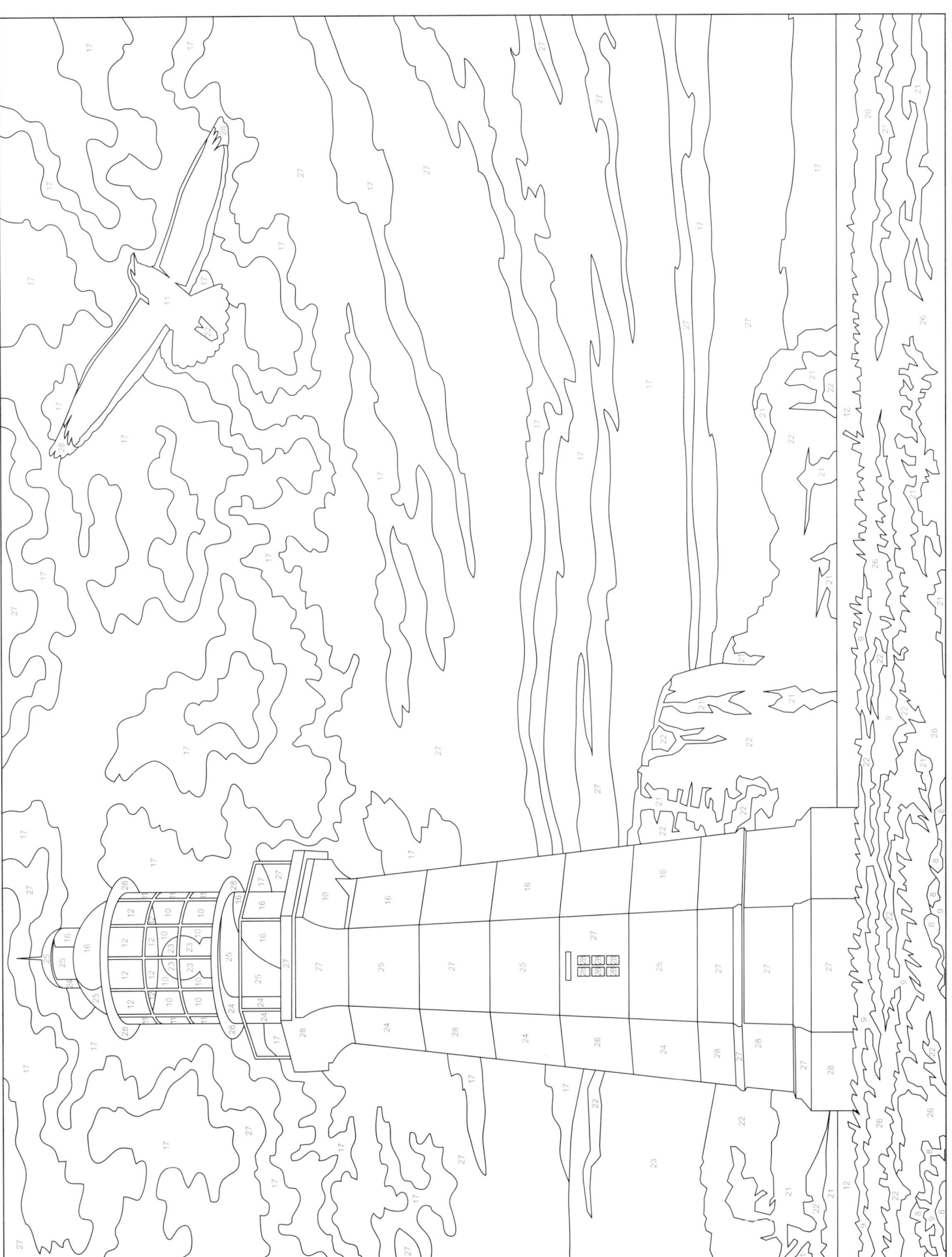

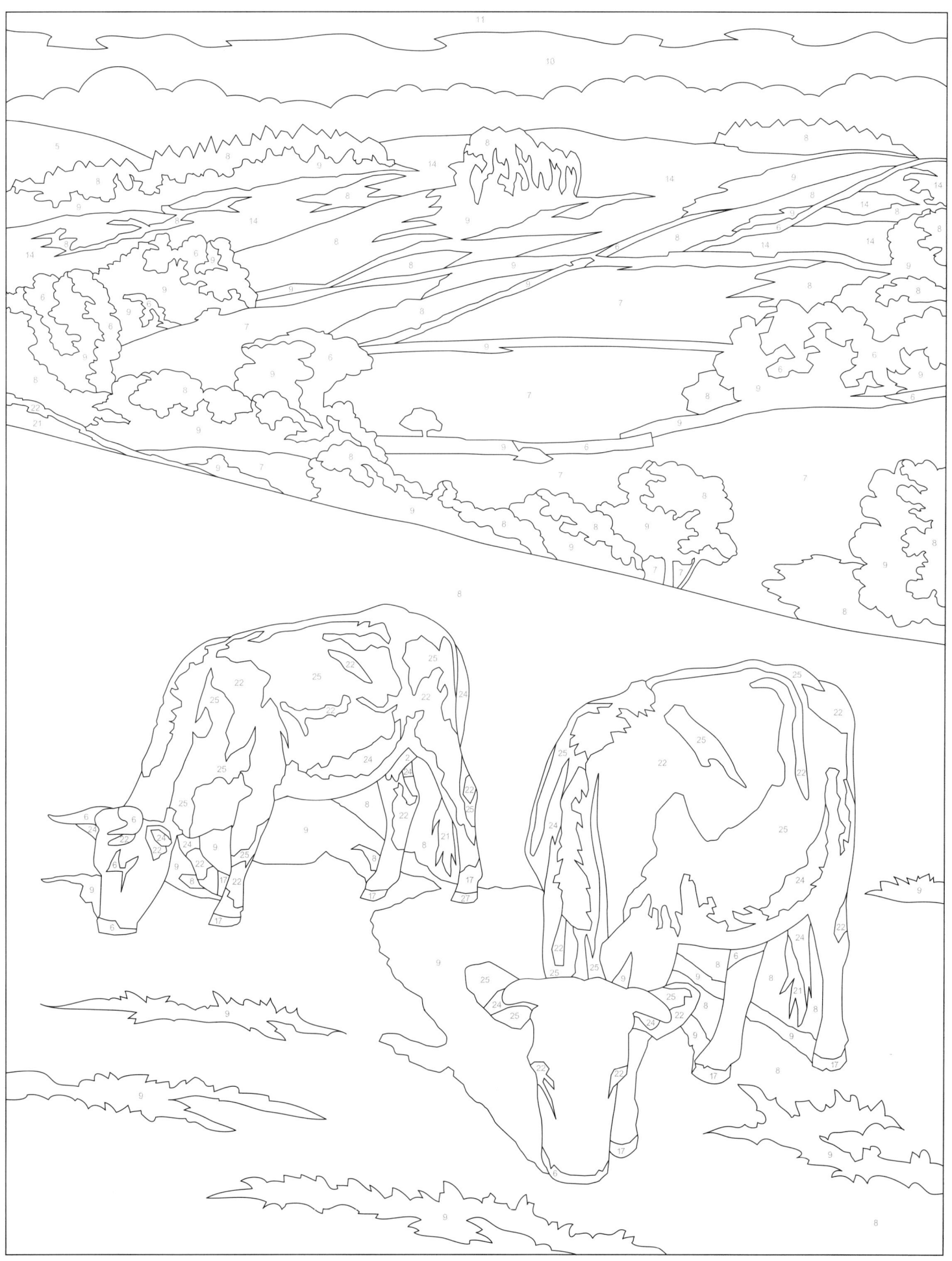

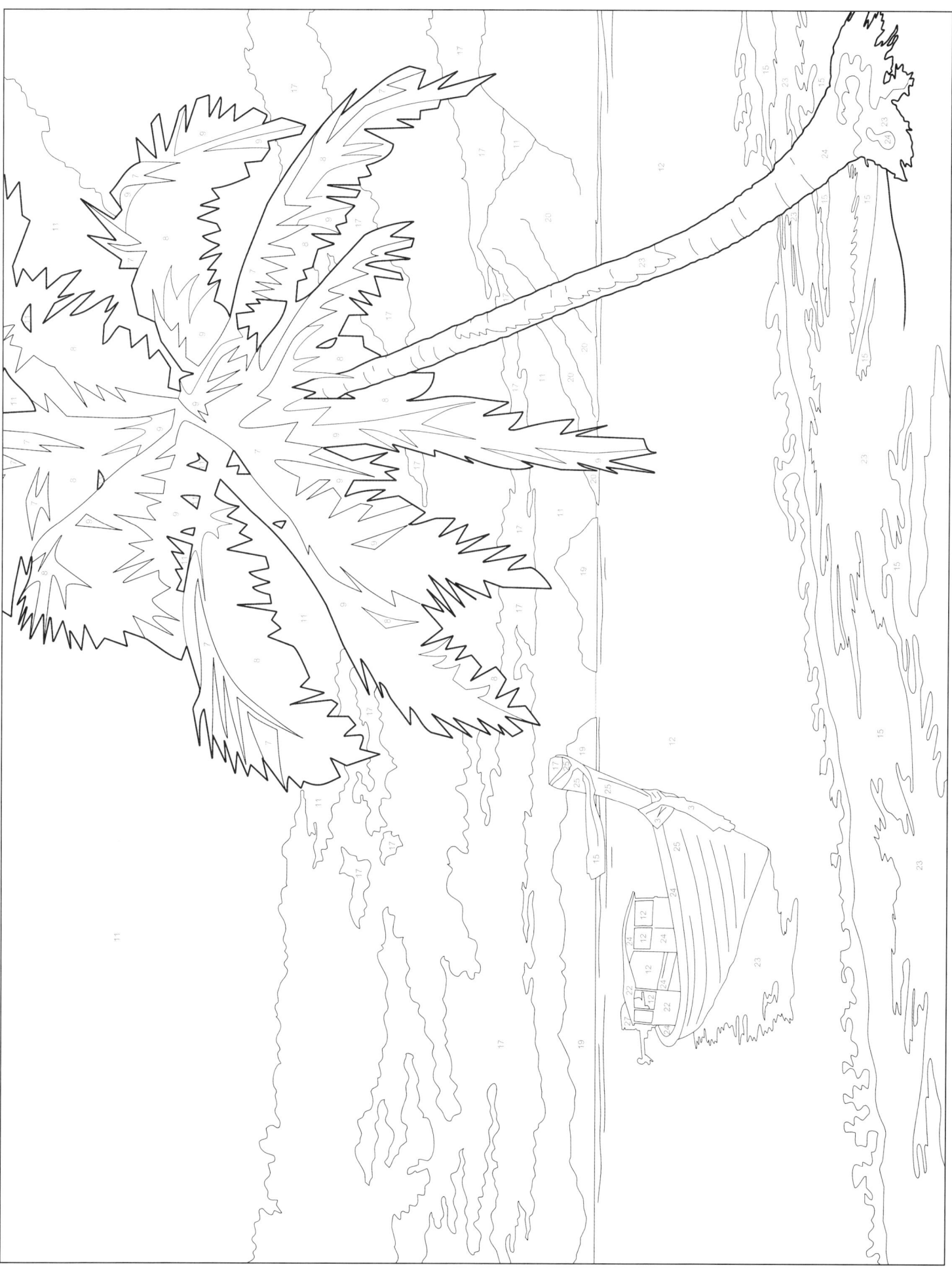

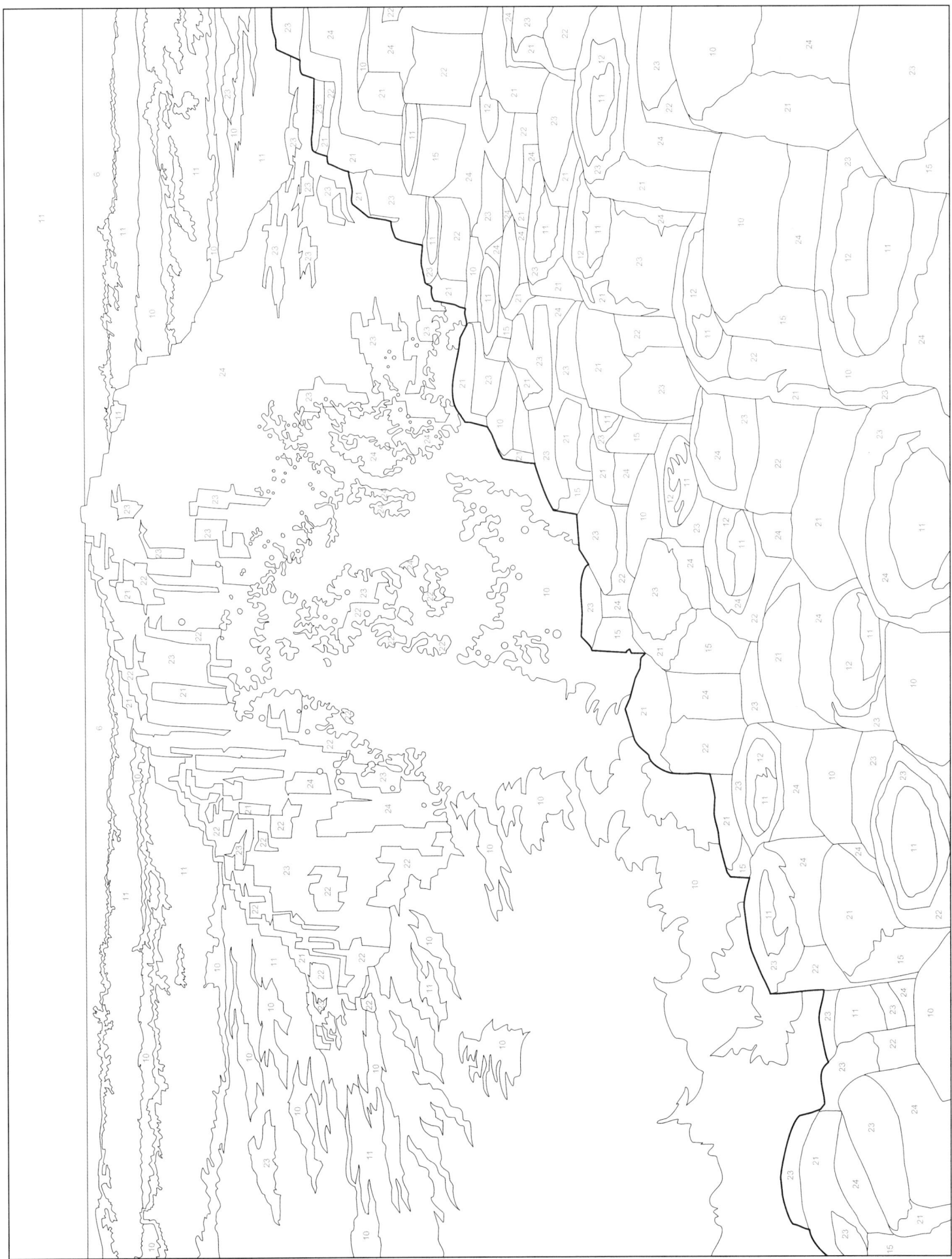

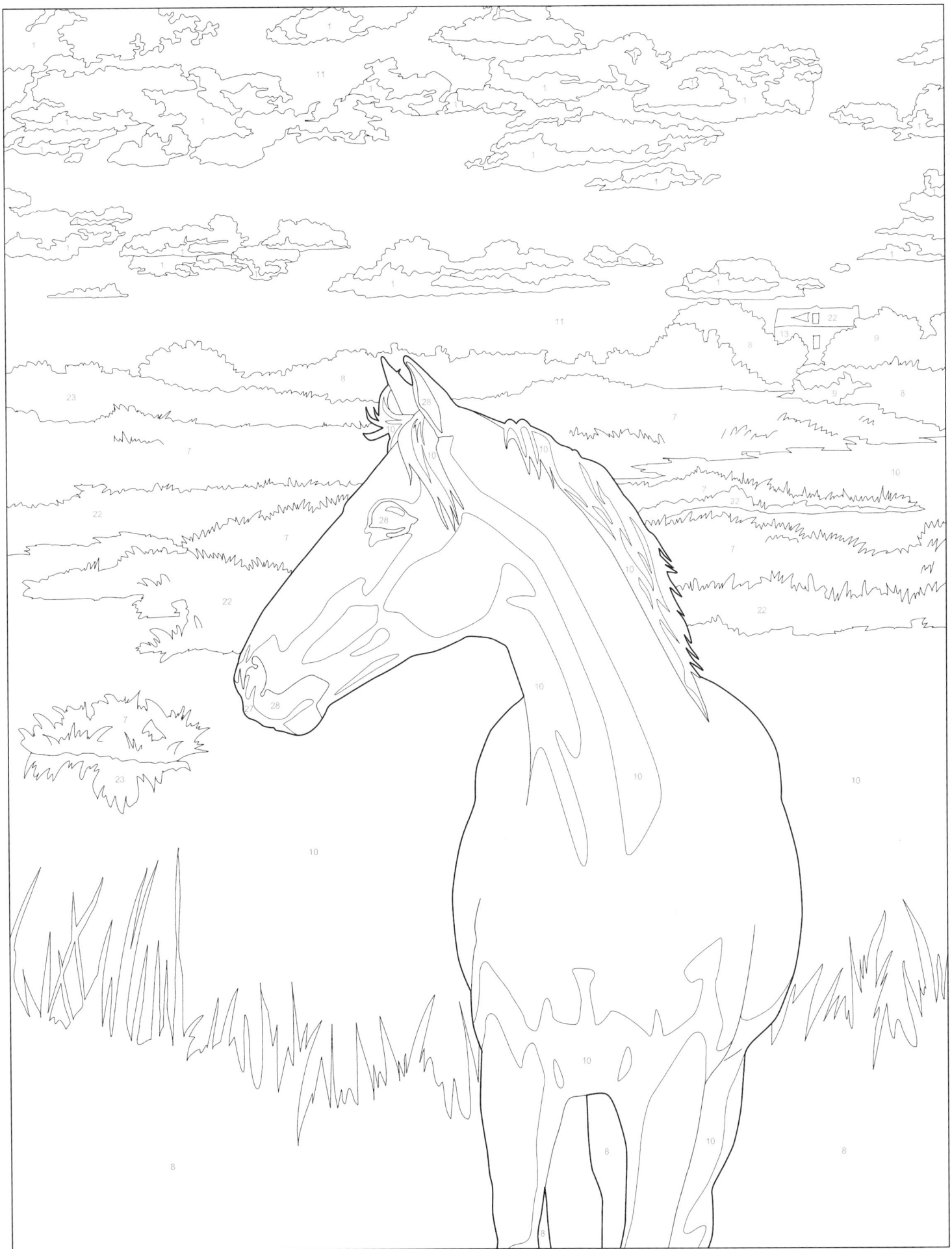

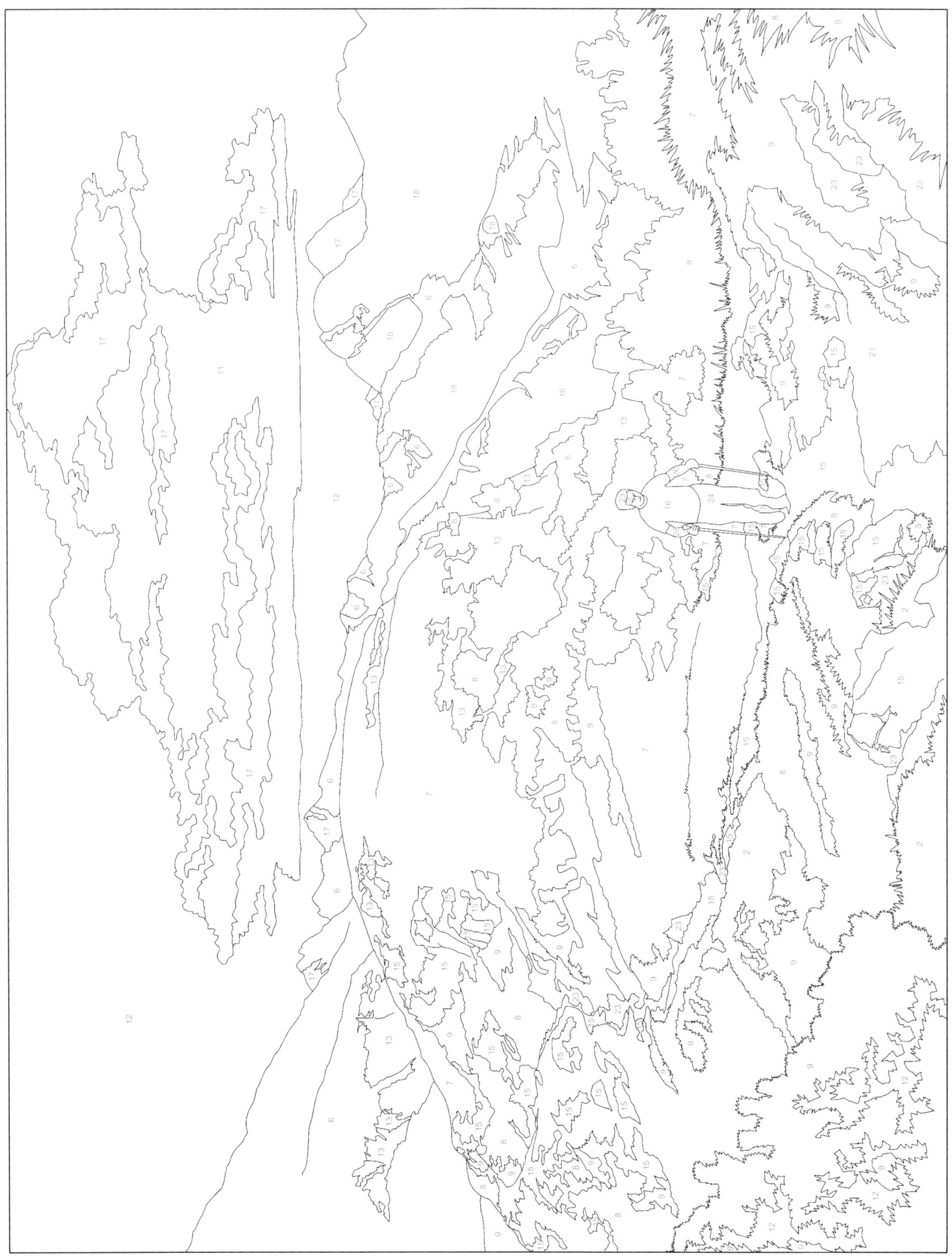

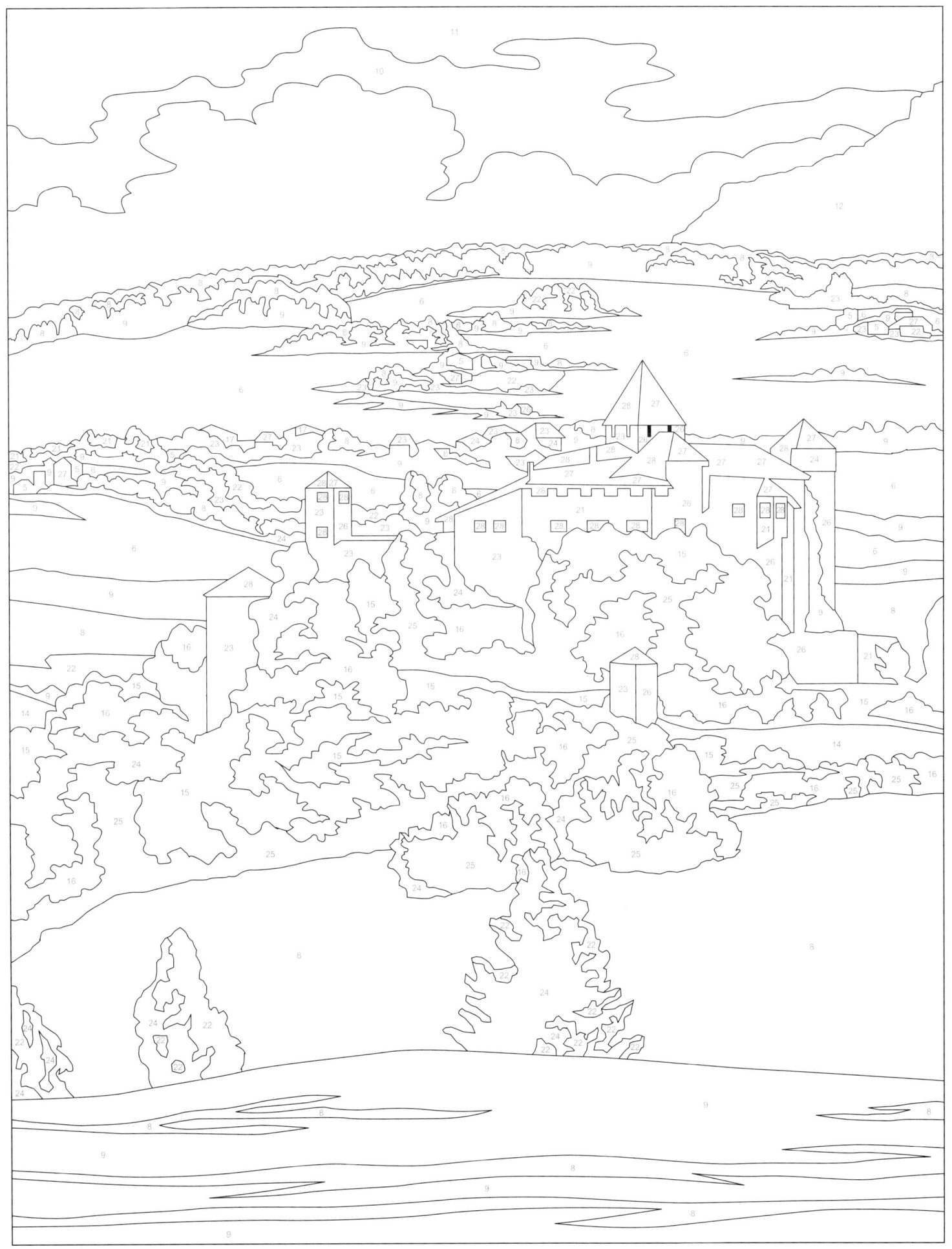

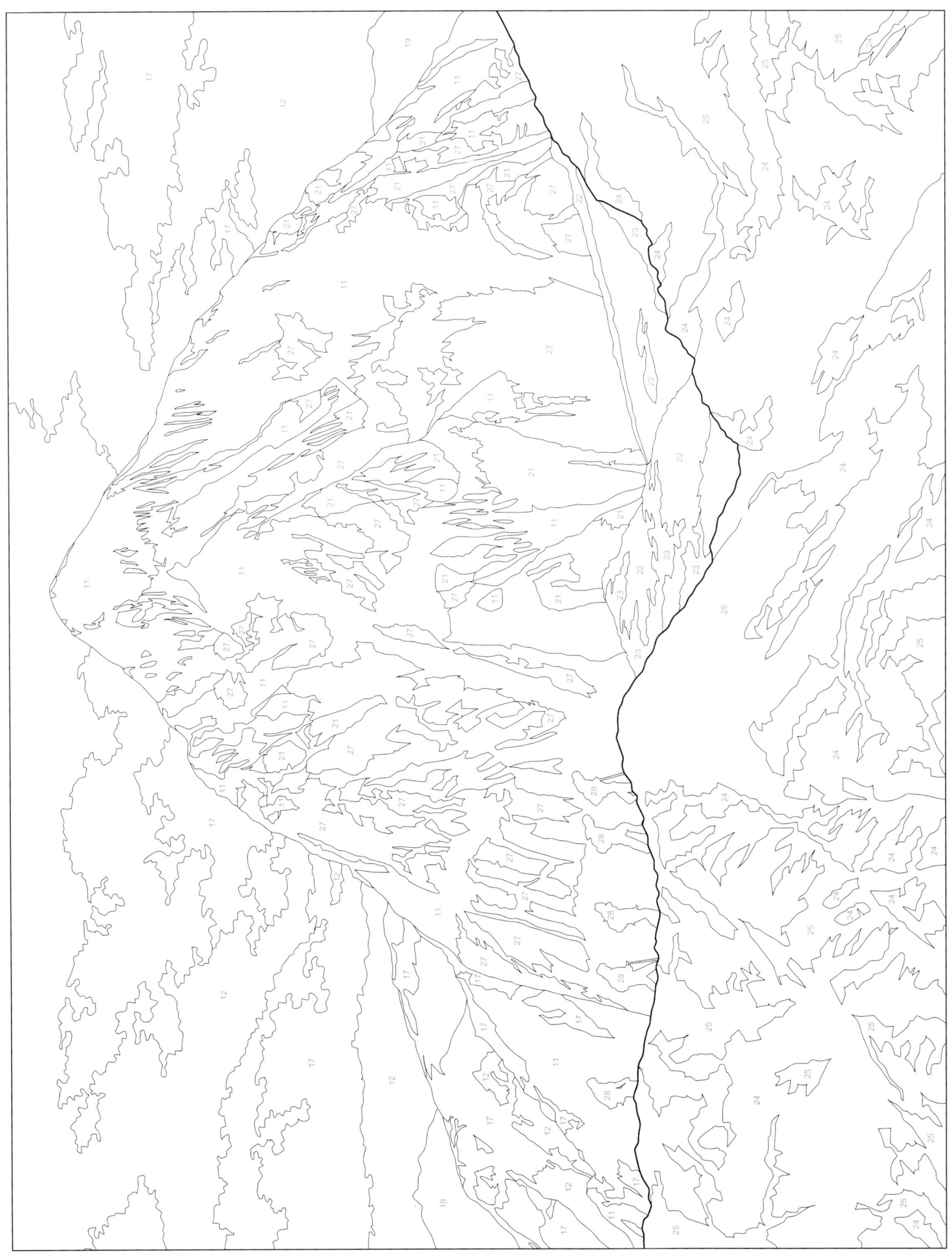

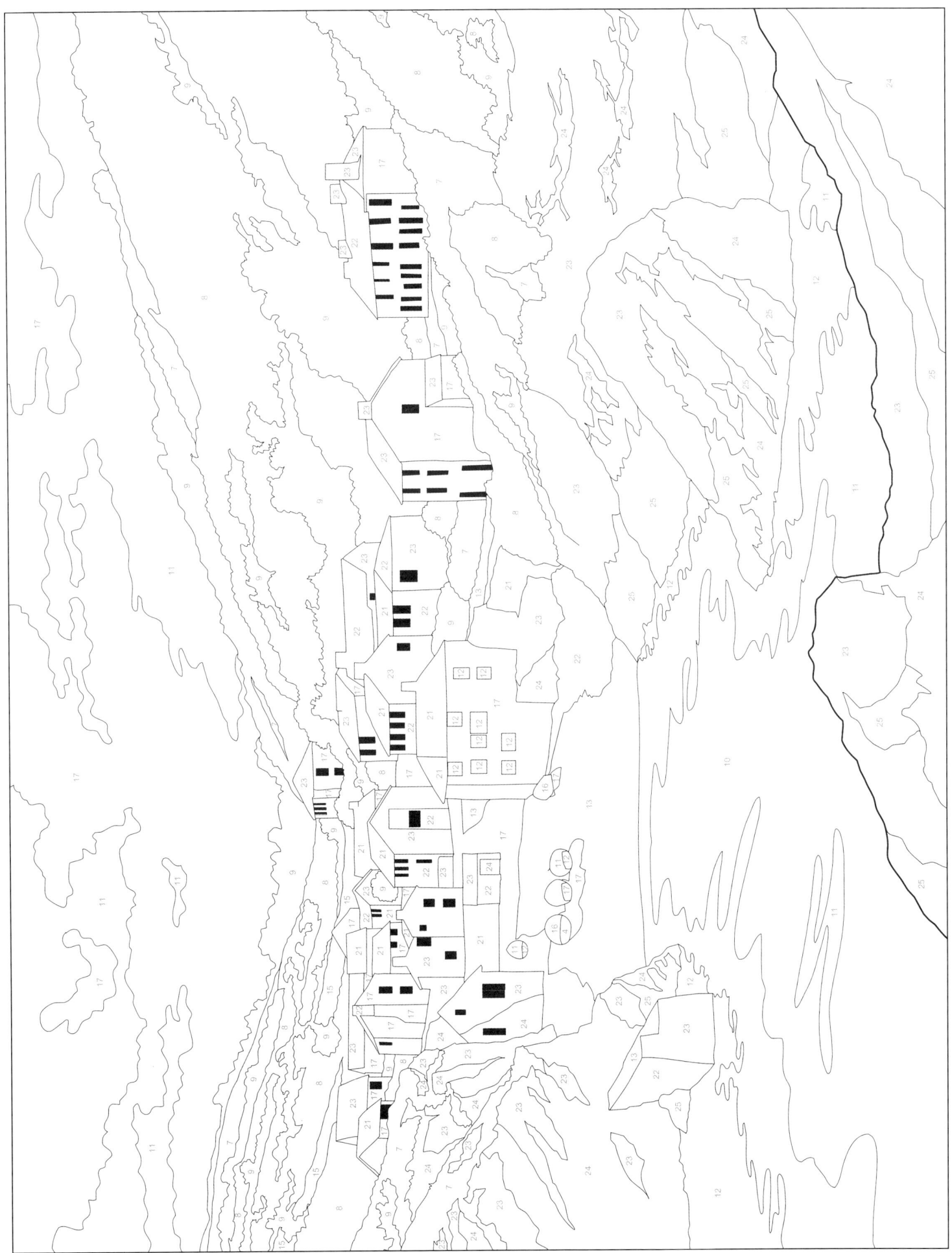

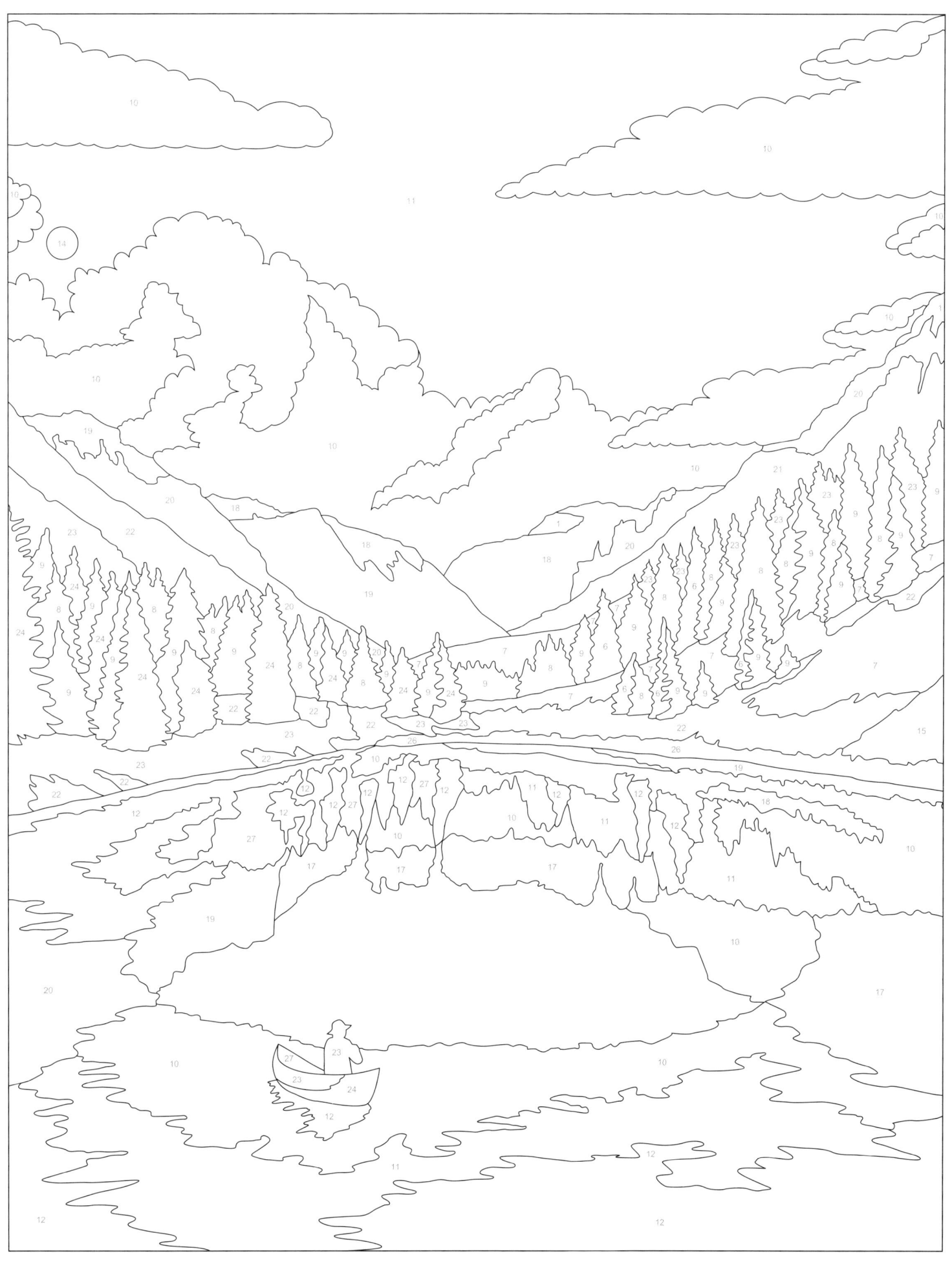

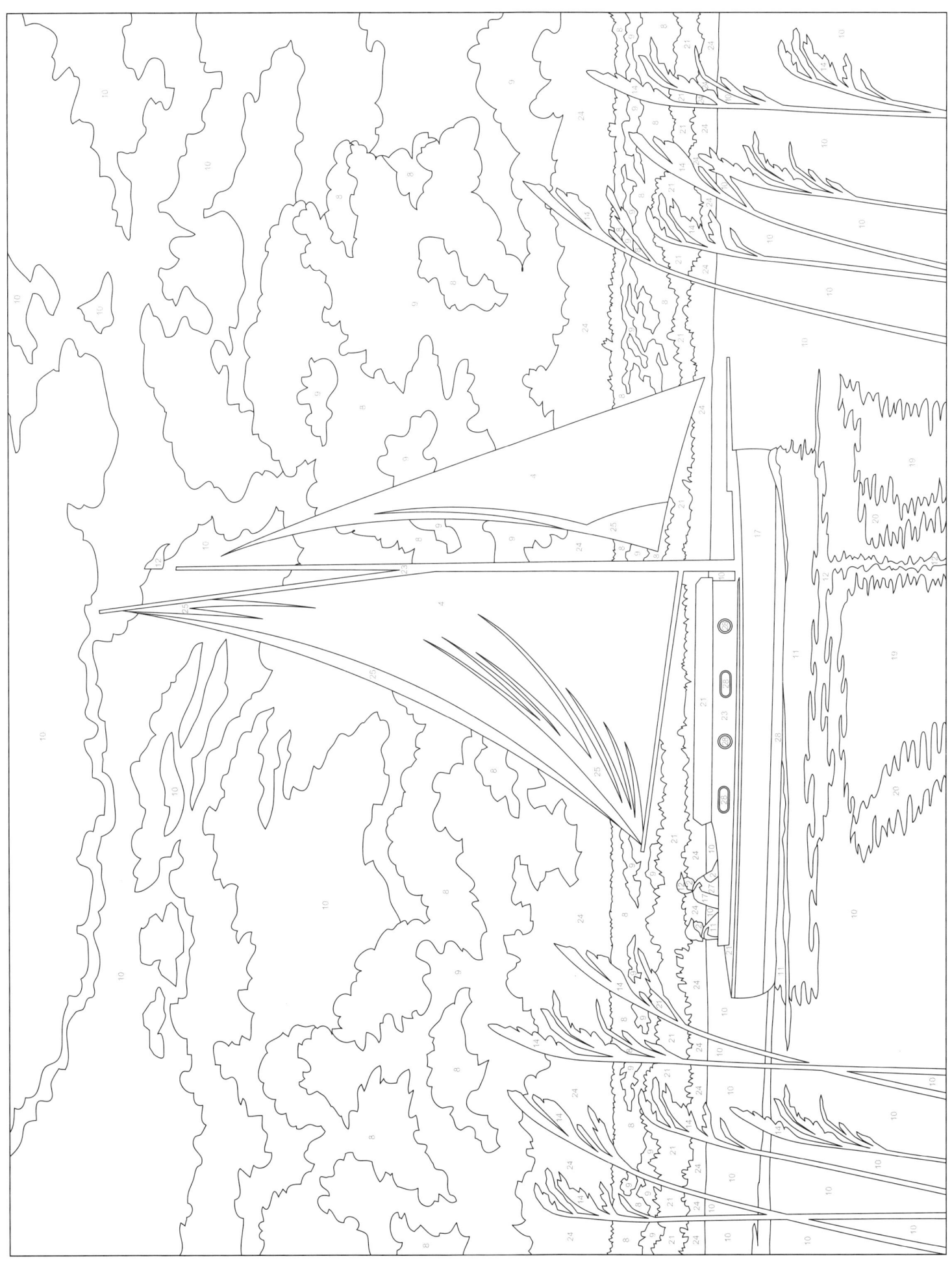

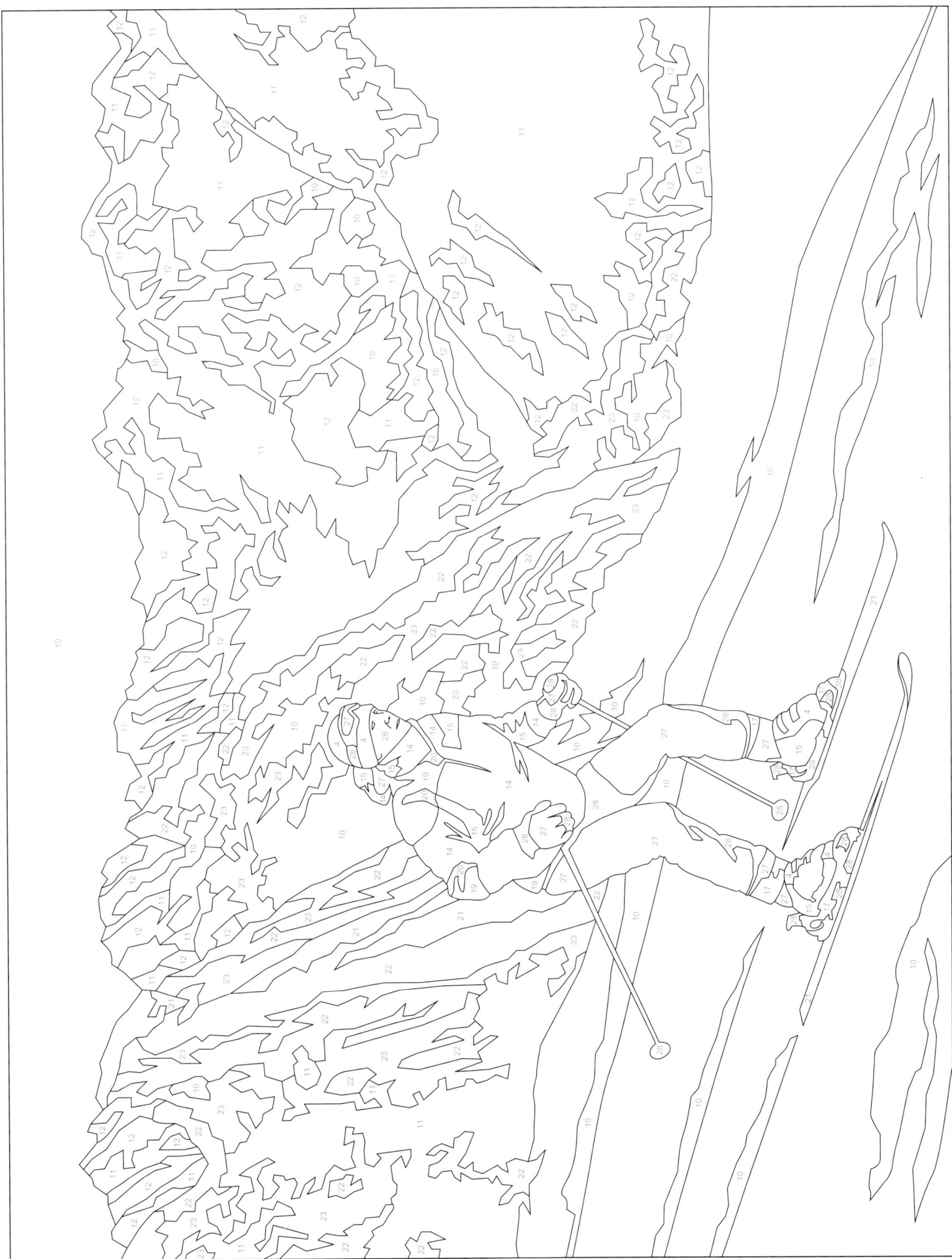

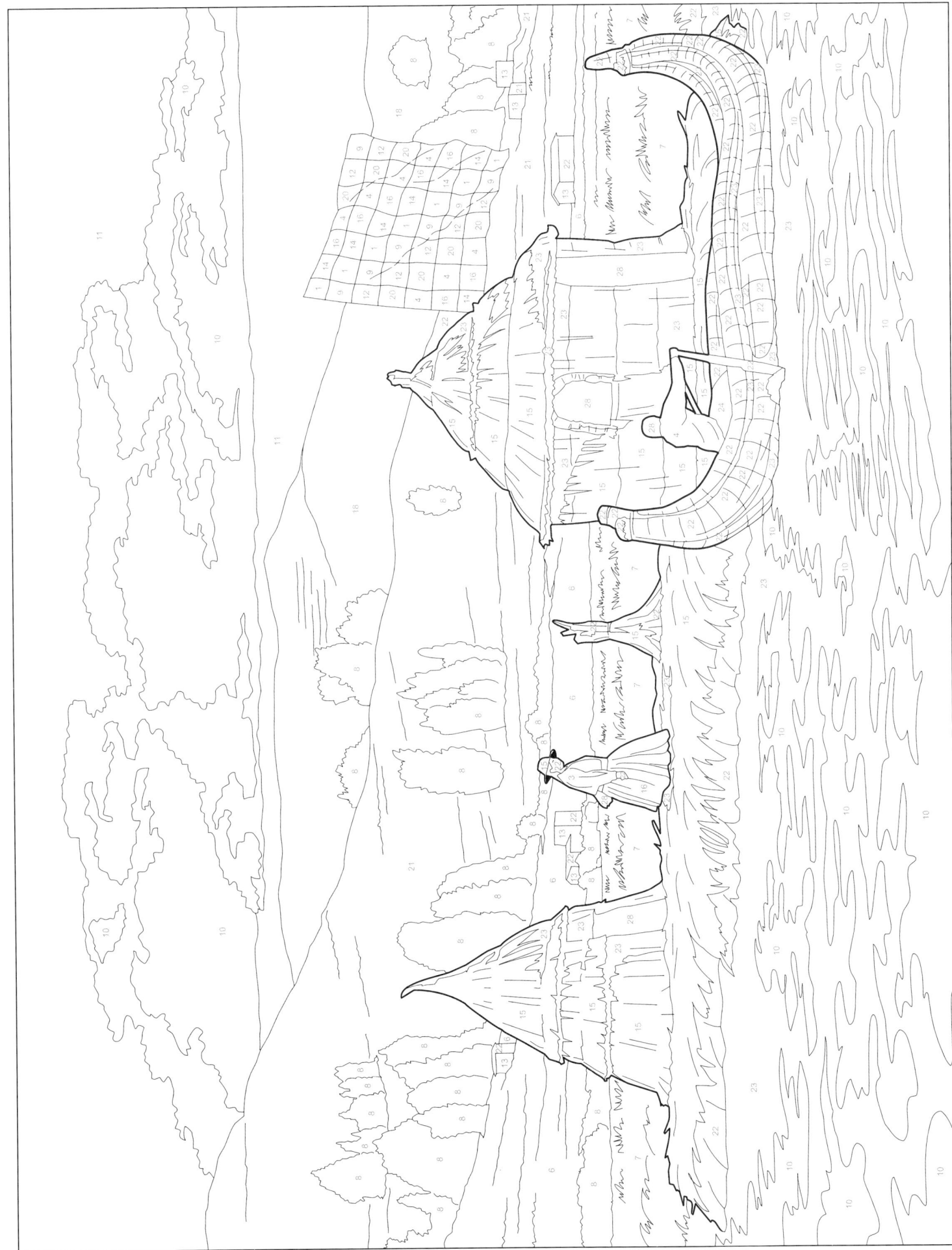

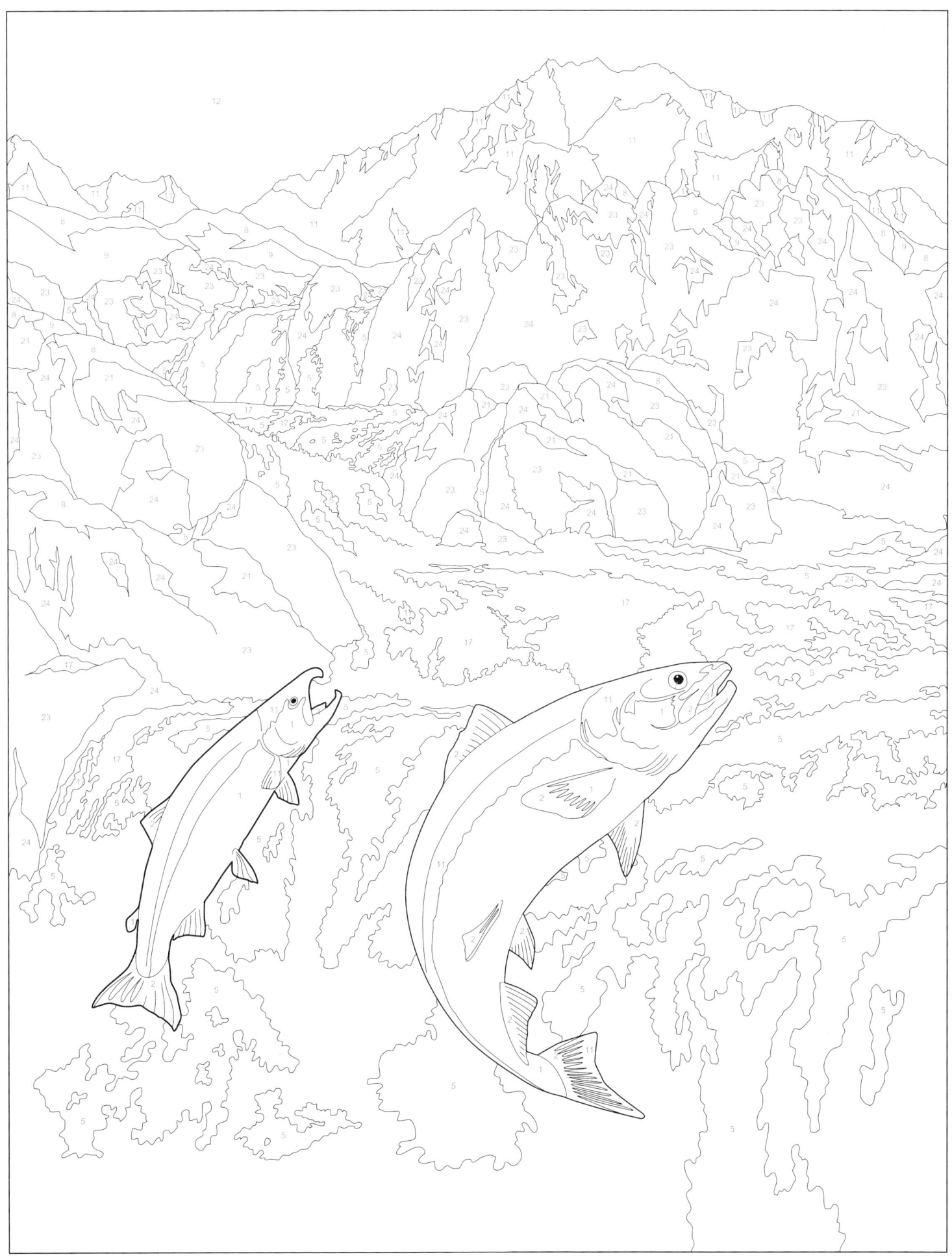

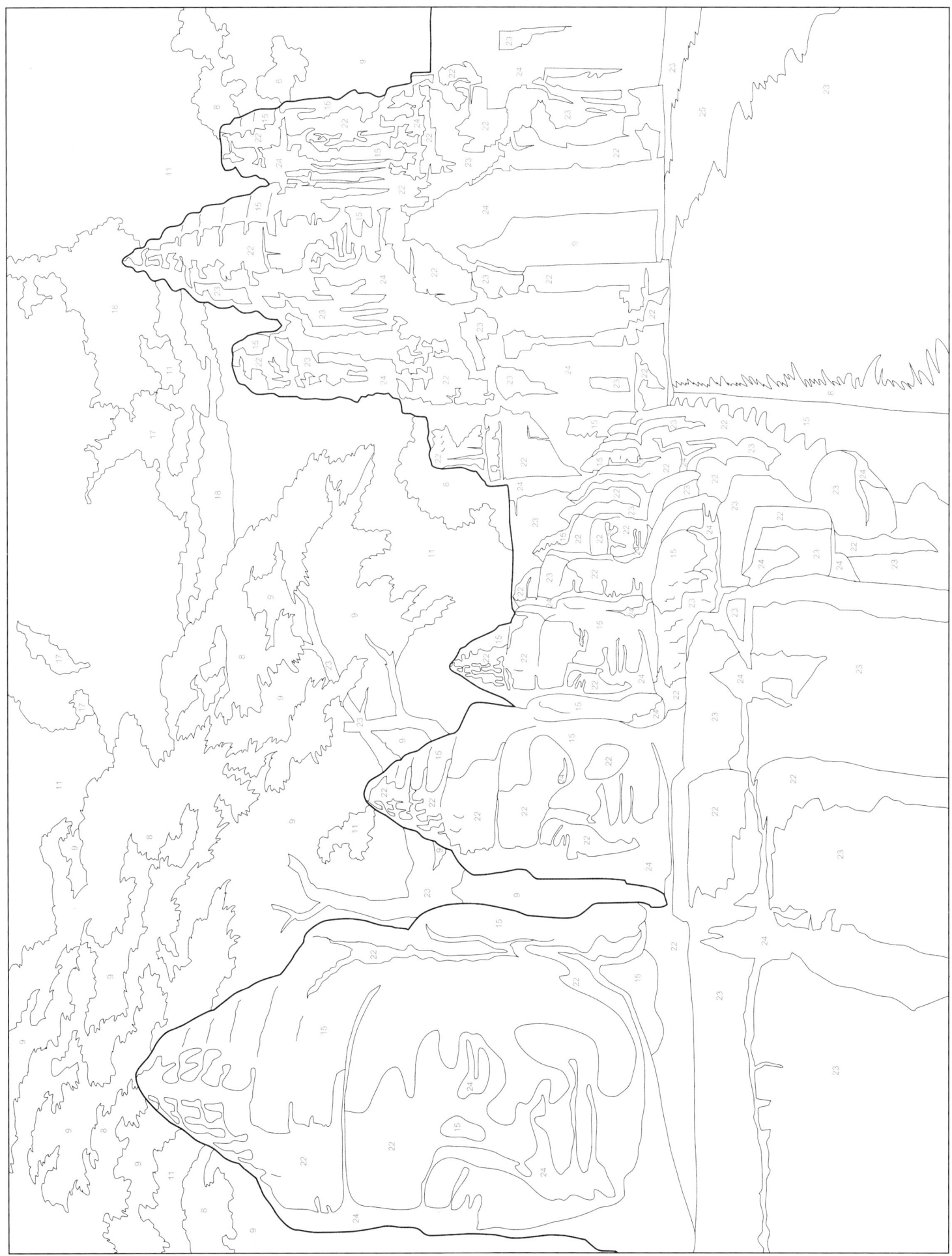

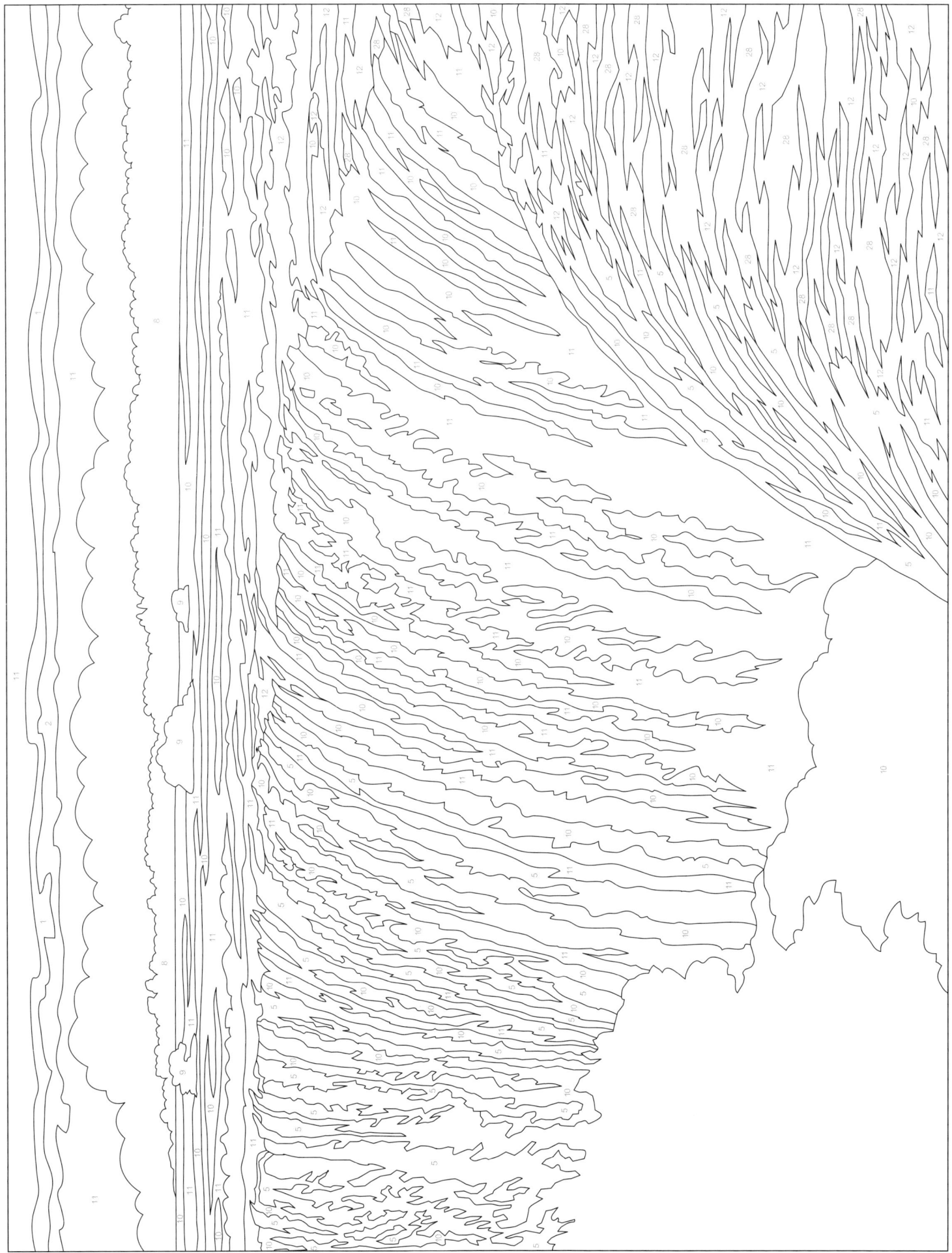

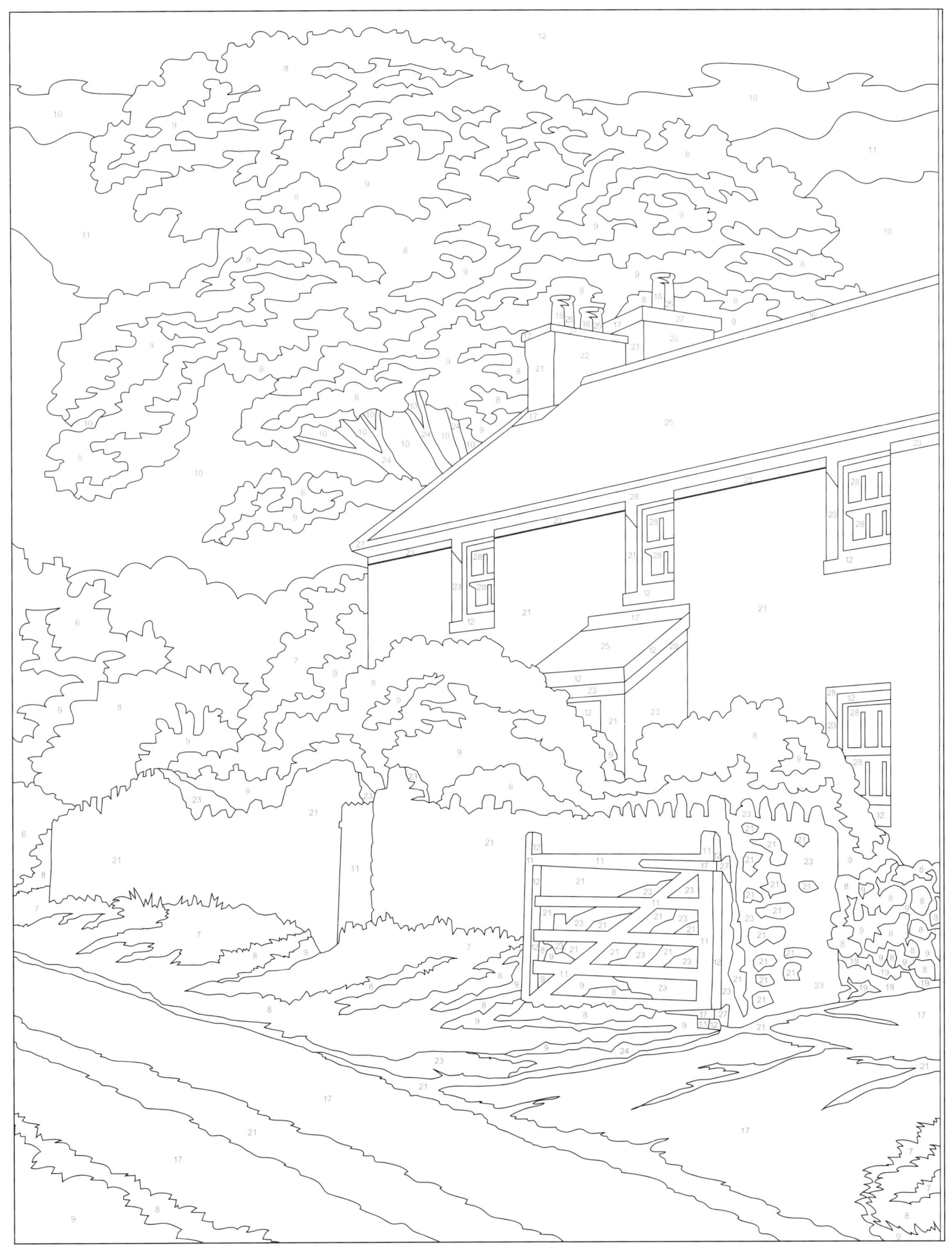